PUNCTUATION 101

101

A fiction writer's guide to getting it right

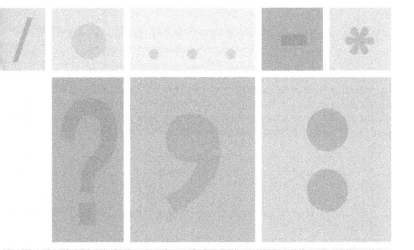

PUNCTUATION

101

A fiction writer's guide
to getting it right

Jill Williamson

Parts of this book originally appeared, in slightly different form, on www.goteenwriters.com, and were copyrighted in 2011, 2012, and 2013 by Jill Williamson.

The author is represented by MacGregor & Luedeke Literary Inc. of Hillsboro, OR.

Cover Designer: Jill Williamson

International Standard Book Number: 978-0-9985230-1-9

Printed in the United States of America

To Deborah, Lisa, and Tracie
for all your help.

TABLE OF CONTENTS

Part 2: Everything Else

Part 3: The Art of Punctuating

INTRODUCTION

One of the hardest things for beginning writers to learn is how to get the story they see in their head out onto the page—the same way they see it in their heads. This is a tricky art form called the craft of writing, and doing it well takes a lot of practice.

Punctuation marks are signals to readers that tell them when to pause or stop and when to change the inflection of a character's voice. Learning to use punctuation correctly will greatly improve your writing craft because written words alone cannot create volume, tone, or emotion. Correct punctuation will also guide your readers through your story so they can understand what you want to say and the way you want them to experience what you say.

Punctuation has never been one of my favorite subjects, but since I wanted to become a published (and professional) author, I needed to learn to do it right.

And so do you.

One mistake in your submission to a literary agent or editor won't likely get you rejected, but if your manuscript is filled with punctuation errors, an agent or editor won't keep reading. They will reject you.

If you want to be treated like a professional, learn what you need to learn to bear that distinction.

From 2011 through 2013, I wrote on the Go Teen Writers blog a series of posts titled *Punctuation 101*. In each post, I tackled one punctuation topic and taught how it related to the specific craft of writing fiction. Some punctuation rules are different if you are writing screenplays or nonfiction articles for magazines or newspapers. This book won't help you with those mediums. This book is for writers of fiction.

This book also won't be 100 percent accurate to help you with a term paper, which most often reference MLA (Modern Language Association) style. Check with your teachers to see which style they want you to use for each assignment. Don't assume! If it will help you get a better grade, make your teachers happy by doing it their way.

But if you are writing a novel that you hope to publish in the United States of America, you should find everything you need to know about punctuation (and likely more) in this book. If you're looking to publish a novel in another country, I urge you to find the industry standard for that country.

If you're serious about writing fiction, I also recommend picking up a copy of *The Chicago Manual of Style*. It's the publishing industry's standard reference guide for works of fiction published in the USA. You don't have to buy the newest version, since the important rules have not changed in quite some time. Add the most recent used copy you can find to your wish list or take a peek at it the next time you visit your local library. It's a great tool to have on your shelf. Until then, this little book should tide you over.

Let's start punctuating, shall we?

Jill

PART 1

What Every Fiction Writer Needs to Know

1
Breaking the Rules

This is a book of rules.

Boo, right?

Writing fiction should be fun and creative. Rules only bog down authors and stifle their creativity.

Not so.

The truth is, consistently using incorrect punctuation could keep you from being published by a traditional publishing house. And if you're an indie author, misusing punctuation will likely earn you some negative book reviews online.

Part of respecting your dream of being a novelist is learning the rules of the English language (or whatever language you're writing in), and that includes learning correct punctuation.

Once you learn the rules and understand them, you're welcome to break them if you have good reason. I do. Here are some ways that I consistently break the rules.

I love sentence fragments. Because they're real. They're how people talk. But they're incomplete sentences. Yet when I write fiction, I use sentence fragments all the time because I like to write in deep points of view that get inside characters' heads.

I tend not to break punctuation rules very often, however, because punctuation is meant to be invisible. It's a guide to the reader, and I want readers to be able to smoothly navigate my novels without stumbling.

I have broken punctuation rules, though. One example is from my *Mission League* novels in which I show texts between two characters. Grace always misspells words and uses twenty exclamation points when she texts, and I felt it was important to show the reader what that looks like and how much it puzzles my main character.

This is a book of rules. Learn these rules and use them, but if you have a good reason to break a rule, go for it. And if any of these terms confuse you or I neglect to define something, don't just wonder, Google it. The internet is your friend when it comes to this subject.

There are a lot of punctuation marks out there. The fact that a type of punctuation exists is not reason enough for you to use it in your novel. Case in point, the section sign: §

Punctuation is meant to be an invisible guide for the reader to navigate a group of words on a page. If your punctuation gets too fancy or veers too far from the norm, that unfamiliar symbol or oddball usage is going to pull your reader out of the story as they ponder what on earth it's supposed to mean.

Pulling your reader out of the story is a bad thing. Novelists want readers immersed in their stories, turning pages until the wee hours of the morning. We want to entertain.

So keep things simple, and don't get fancy unless you have good reason. There is rarely a good reason to use an asterism, a section sign, or an interrobang in a novel.

Trust me.

2
Some Basics

You don't need to know every grammar term to write a great novel, but if I'm going to teach you about punctuation, I'm going to have to use some textbook words like *subjunctive* and *appositive*. This chapter is a need-to-know glossary of sorts to help you understand a few terms up front.

Sentence Types
Throughout this book, I will occasionally refer to different types of sentences. There are four sentence types in the English language:

Declarative
Imperative
Interrogative
Exclamatory

A declarative sentence makes a statement or expresses an opinion. A declarative sentence almost always ends with a period.

An imperative sentence gives a request or makes a command. Imperative sentences usually end in a period but sometimes end in an exclamation point.

An interrogative sentence asks a question and almost always ends in a question mark.

And finally, an exclamatory sentence expresses great emotion and often ends in an exclamation point.

Anything that isn't a complete sentence is a fragment.

What does "set in Roman" mean?

The phrase "set in Roman" simply means regular text that is not italicized, bolded, or anything out of the norm.

What's the difference between Roman numerals, Arabic numerals, cardinal numbers, and ordinal numbers?

There are a lot of different ways to write numbers. Here is how it all works.

Roman numerals are letters that represent numbers as part of the Roman numerical system. They are I for 1, V for 5, X for 10, L for 50, C for 100, D for 500, and M for 1,000.

Arabic numerals replaced Roman numerals during the middle ages. They are 0, 1, 2, 3, 4, 5, 6, 7, 8, 9.

Cardinal numbers denote quantity. They

can be spelled out (one, two, three, seventy-eight) or written in numeral form (5, 86, 249).

Ordinal numbers define something's place in a series (first, second, third, fifty-ninth).

What is a clause?

A clause is a group of words that contain a subject and a verb. Clauses that can stand on their own are called *independent* or *main* clauses. Clauses that cannot stand on their own are called *dependent* or *subordinate* clauses. A dependent clause depends on the rest of the sentence for meaning.

Here are some examples of independent clauses.

She wrote.
I love to read.
Irene looked at the ring.[1]
He didn't say what kind of book his sister is writing.
Katie went to a writers conference by herself.
The new bookstore has a huge teen section.
The coach's voice scraped like sandpaper against his
    ears.[2]

Here are some examples of sentences with dependent clauses. I underlined those clauses.

She will learn <u>whatever is necessary</u> to finish her book.
The book <u>that she wrote</u> was her second novel.
Everyone went to a movie <u>while she continued writing</u>.
<u>If she can finish her novel before the conference</u>, she
    will pitch the idea to an agent.
<u>After months of writing</u>, she finally finished her book.

<u>Since no one else signed up</u>, she got the appointment.
<u>When she met with the agent</u>, he liked her idea and
   asked her to send him the full manuscript.
<u>Because she missed her deadline</u>, her release day was
   delayed.

What is the difference between a coordinating conjunction and a subordinating conjunction?

A coordinating conjunction has one function: to join clauses of equal importance. The acronym FANBOYS is a nifty way to help you remember the most common coordinating conjunctions: for, and, nor, but, or, yet, so. Notice in the examples below how the clauses connected by each coordinating conjunction have the same construction.

I went to the post office and to the bank.
She took her finger out of her mouth and looked at me. [3]
I love *Doctor Who* but hate *Torchwood*.
Andy has a brand new car, yet he never drives it.

Dependent (subordinate) clauses begin with a subordinating conjunction. A dependent clause must be attached to a main clause or it will be a sentence fragment. When a dependent clause comes at the beginning of the sentence, you need a comma. If it comes later in the sentence, you do not need a comma.

Here is a list of several subordinating conjunctions:

after	once	whenever
although	provided that	where
as	rather than	whereas
because	since	where if
before	so that	wherever
even if	than	whether
even though	that	which
if	though	while
in order that	unless	who
just as	until	whoever
now that	when	why

Let's look again at some of those sentences with dependent clauses, this time underlining the subordinating conjunctions.

She will learn whatever is necessary to finish her book.
The book that she wrote was her second novel.
Everyone went to a movie while she continued writing.
If she can finish her novel before the conference, she
    will pitch the idea to an agent.
After months of writing, she finally finished her book.
Since no one else signed up, she got the appointment.

What are misplaced and dangling modifiers?

A modifier changes something in a sentence. Misplaced modifiers unintentionally change the meaning of the wrong thing. Dangling modifiers are trying to change the meaning of something that isn't even in the sentence. Both create confusion and sometimes physical impossibilities.

What is an appositive?

An appositive is a noun, noun phrase, pronoun, or pronoun phrase that is put next to another noun, noun phrase, pronoun, or pronoun phrase in order to rename, redefine, further explain, or to provide more information. (Whew!)

If that was totally confusing, basically, an appositive is a word or phrase that redefines another word or phrase.

Appositives can be any number of words. They are usually set apart with a pair of commas or parentheses. If you want to emphasize the information, you could also use a single colon, as long as the text preceding it is a complete sentence, or an em dash, as long as the appositive comes directly after the noun it's redefining.

An appositive can come at the beginning, the middle, or the end of a sentence. If you're using two em dashes in the middle of a sentence, the first one must be next to the word or phrase you're describing.

My brother, Joe, went to college this week.
The book, a thick tome with gilded pages, is begging to be read.
My cat, a ten-year-old Persian, looks like it's going bald.
The new kid (a tall, dark-eyed, muscular football player) sat by me at lunch.
Claustrophobia—stuck in the middle seat on a trans-Atlantic flight—was making this flight seem longer.

Before I can leave for vacation, I must do <u>one important task: shut the garage door</u>.

Try rewriting your sentence by moving the appositive around. Remember, it can come at the beginning, the middle, or the end.

<u>Katie, a talented young author</u>, pitched her story to an agent and got a request to send the full manuscript.

Excited by the news, the conference director praised <u>Katie, a talented young author</u> who pitched her story to an agent and got a request to send the full manuscript.

The agent requested a full manuscript from <u>Katie, a talented young author</u>.

3
Common Mistakes in Fiction

The following are punctuation mistakes I've seen over and over in manuscripts I've read at writing conferences and in my experience as an editor. I've even found these errors in published novels—some in bestselling novels. So, take heart. Even famous authors and/or their editors make mistakes. We're all human, after all.

I will go over many of these mistakes again in each appropriate chapter, but I thought it might be useful to have this list right up front and handy.

Don't use a comma with a coordinating conjunction to set off a dependent clause.

One of the most common mistakes I see in fiction manuscripts is when authors use a comma with a coordinating conjunction to set off a dependent clause.

Incorrect: Michael let the dog inside, and gave it a bath.

The comma in that example is incorrect because the clause "gave it a bath" is not a complete sentence on its own. It depends on the first part of the sentence to make sense.

Correct: Michael let the dog inside and gave it a bath.

Don't create absurd scenarios due to misplaced and/or dangling modifiers.

Modifying phrases placed at the front of a sentence that are set off with a comma are often grammatically incorrect and result in ridiculous statements.

Incorrect: Having been finished last night, Megan could wear her homemade dress to prom.

Since "having been finished last night" is next to Megan in the sentence, the words mean that Megan was finished last night, not the dress. Let's look at another.

Incorrect: Looking down the road, a cloud of dust obscured the approaching vehicle.

The above sentence does not identify a person looking down the road, and since the modifier, "looking down the road," is next to "a cloud of dust," the sentence suggests that the cloud is looking down the road.

Sometimes these types of sentences can work. When editing, take a careful look at your modifying phrases to see whether they can remain as is or if they need to be rewritten.

Correct: Having finished making the dress last night, Megan could wear it to prom.

Correct: Looking down the road, I saw nothing but a cloud of dust obscuring the approaching vehicle.

Correct: I looked down the road but saw nothing but a cloud of dust obscuring the approaching vehicle.

Don't forget to use commas to set off a name or title used in direct address.

When a name or title is used in direct address, it means someone is being spoken to, and that name must be set off with commas. You need a comma on both sides, unless the name starts or ends the sentence. If you forget one or more commas, it is incorrect.

Incorrect: Mom can you come here?
Correct: Mom, can you come here?

Incorrect: I don't want to talk about it Jason.
Correct: I don't want to talk about it, Jason.

Incorrect: Come here Kaitlyn so I can see you.
Incorrect: Come here, Kaitlyn so I can see you.
Incorrect: Come here Kaitlyn, so I can see you.
Correct: Come here, Kaitlyn, so I can see you.

Don't create comma splices.

A comma splice incorrectly joins two independent clauses with a comma. This is a no-no. Comma splices can be fixed in the following ways: (1) by breaking the sentence into two separate sentences, (2) by adding a conjunction after the comma, (3) by adding a subordinating conjunction and rewording the sentence, or (4) by changing the comma to a semicolon, but only if the two sentences are closely related in subject matter.

Incorrect: My family travels to California every year, we go to Disneyland and the beach.

Correct (by breaking the sentence in two): My family travels to California every year. We go to Disneyland and the beach.

Correct (by adding a coordinating conjunction after the comma): My family travels to California every year, and we go to Disneyland and the beach.

Correct (by adding a subordinating conjunction and a comma): Whenever my family travels to California, we go to Disneyland and the beach.

Correct (by changing the comma to a semicolon since these two sentences are related in thought): My family travels to California every year; we go to Disneyland and the beach.

Don't create a run-on (fused) sentence.

A run-on or fused sentence has two main clauses joined with no punctuation. A run-on sentence can be fixed in the same four ways as a comma splice, as long as the clauses are like enough in thought to use a semicolon.

Incorrect: Grandpa still plays baseball he uses the same glove he used in college.

Correct (by breaking the sentence in two): Grandpa still plays baseball. He uses the same glove he used in college.

Correct (by adding a coordinating conjunction after the comma): Grandpa still plays baseball, and he uses the same glove he used in college.

Correct (by adding a subordinating conjunction and a comma): When Grandpa plays baseball, he uses the same glove he used in college.

Correct (by changing the comma to a semicolon since these two sentences are related in thought): Grandpa still plays baseball; he uses the same glove he used in college.

All of these rules do not mean that an author cannot use a run-on sentence effectively. In the following example from *A Tale of Two Cities*, Charles Dickens writes a run-on sentence that is so powerful and engaging that its being incorrect just doesn't matter.[1]

It was the best of times, it was the worst of times, it was the age of wisdom, it was the age of foolishness, it was the epoch of belief, it was the epoch of incredulity, it was the season of Light, it was the season of Darkness, it was the spring of hope, it was the winter of despair, we had everything before us, we had nothing before us, we were all going direct to Heaven, we were all going direct the other way—in short, the period was so far like the present period, that some of the noisiest authorities insisted on its being received, for good or evil, in the superlative degree of comparison only.

Don't add commas just so the reader can pause for a breath.

It's not a good idea to try to be clever with punctuation until you've learned the rules. Once you learn to use punctuation correctly, I think you'll find that there are plenty of places for the reader to pause and take a breath. At that point, if you want to add or take away commas for clarity, artistic reasons, or to create a certain effect, go for it.

I have found, though, that many authors insert a comma when what they really want to use is an ellipsis. If you want to show a great pause or someone trailing off while they think or search for the right word . . . an ellipsis is the way to do that.

Don't use incorrect dialogue tags.

I see lots of errors in the punctuating of dialogue, so many, in fact, that I've devoted Chapter 14 to the subject.

Correctly capitalize kinship names.

Kinship names are lowercase unless they are being used in place of, as part of, or as all of a personal name. If you are using a title like *dad* or *aunt* with a pronoun (my, his, your), then *dad* or *aunt* will be lowercase. But if you're using *Dad* as a name or *aunt* with a name (Aunt Mary), then the titles will be capitalized.

Did you see <u>my mom</u> and <u>dad</u>?
Because <u>Mom</u> said I could go.
Is <u>your dad</u> coming?
Why won't you answer, <u>Dad</u>?
The <u>Weasley</u> twins are trouble.
I emailed <u>Uncle Steve</u> yesterday.
Did you know <u>my aunt Janet</u> lives in Arizona?
My boyfriend's basketball <u>coach</u> is so mean.
"Put me in the game, <u>Coach</u>!"

Don't use quotation marks for emphasis.

Many authors put quotation marks around a word to add emphasis, but that is incorrect. Instead, use *italics* to emphasize.

Incorrect: I am "so" tired of Doug calling me.
Correct: I am *so* tired of Doug calling me.

Don't confuse hyphens, em dashes, en dashes, and ellipses.

It's common for authors to mix up hyphens with dashes and dashes with ellipses, but each has its proper usage.

Hyphens (-), en dashes (–), and em dashes (—) look very similar and technically only differ by the length of the dash. In a sentence, however, they couldn't be more different. I have chapters that discuss each of these in depth, so make sure you understand when to use each one.

Don't confuse homonyms like it's and its.

Homonyms are easy to confuse. Google "commonly confused homonyms," and you'll find a long list of words to watch out for when writing. More than any other, I see authors mixing up *it's* and *its*. Remember, *it's* is a contraction for *it is*, while *its* is a possessive pronoun. When uncertain which to use, read your sentence and say *"it is"* out loud. If the sentence doesn't make sense, omit the apostrophe.

Incorrect: The bird flew to it's *(it is)* nest.
Correct: The bird flew to its nest.

Don't confuse yeah, yay, and yea.

This is one of my pet peeves. These three words aren't technically homonyms because they don't sound quite the same, nor are they spelled the same, but they are often misused. *Yeah* means *yes* or an affirmative answer. *Yay* is an expression of joy. And *yea* is a yes vote.

Incorrect: Yea! I won!
Correct: Yay! I won!

Incorrect: Yea, I'll be there.
Correct: Yeah, I'll be there.

Incorrect: I voted yeah, but everyone else said nay.
Correct: I voted yea, but everyone else said nay.

Don't use two spaces between sentences.

Back when authors used typewriters, it was common practice to put two spaces between sentences. Now that everyone uses computers, one space between sentences is correct. If you simply can't get used to that, no worries. When you're done with your manuscript, simply add a step before you spell check. Do a Find and Replace from *two spaces* to *one*. That will take care of the problem with the click of a button.

For you screenwriters out there, this rule does not apply. Screenplays still require two spaces between sentences. This punctuation book is for writers of fiction. While many punctuation rules are the same for both mediums, if you're writing screenplays, pick up a copy of *The Hollywood Standard: The Complete and Authoritative Guide to Script Format and Style* by Christopher Riley. It's the go-to reference for anyone writing for the screen.

4
Periods

I used to think periods were the one type of punctuation I couldn't mess up if I tried. I was wrong. While the decision to use a period, question mark, or exclamation point at the end of a sentence is the author's choice, there are rules you should know to help guide your choices. Rules that will help you.

Use a period at the end of a declarative or a mildly imperative sentence.

It doesn't matter whether your sentence is long, short, complete, incomplete, a run-on (which you really should avoid), or a sentence fragment (which are common in fiction). Unless you're asking a question or making an exclamation, a period belongs at the end.

It begins with a house.[1]
Christy spurred the horse into a gallop.

Not so much.
You rat.
I don't get into trouble. Anymore.
Beatrice Quimby's biggest problem was her little sister
Ramona.[2]

Use a period after a polite request.

Polite requests sometimes feel like questions, but since their intent is to give instructions, they're actually imperative sentences. Because of that, and since they don't require an answer, they don't require a question mark.

Confirm your reservation by June 12.
Will the audience please stand for the singing of our
    national anthem.
Take your time and answer truthfully.
Come and visit us when you come back to the city.

Use a period after an indirect question.

An indirect question does not require the use of a question mark.

He wondered where to go next.
Marilla had been wondering where Anne should be
    put to bed.[3]
"Coach wants to know when I can come to practice."
If only he could find someone to ask where to get help.
How she had died was the question on everyone's mind.
He asked himself why.

Abbreviations

Abbreviations are shortened forms of words. Use a period with abbreviations that end in lowercase letters, for example, Mr., Mrs., Dr., etc., a.m., St., Ave., gal., yd., Jan.

Use a period for initials that represent a full name: J. R. R. Tolkien.

Do not use periods for abbreviations that have two or more capital letters: WA, USA, UK, CIA, PhD, GTW.

WHEN I BROKE THE RULES

In my *Mission League* series, Spencer's teacher is Patrick Stopplecamp, but everyone calls him Mr. S. I got tired of putting a period after the S, and when the book was published, my editor agreed to leave it off. Normally, the rule is that you should use a period after a letter that replaces a name, but we chose to ignore that rule for Mr. S and leave off the period.

Acronyms and Initialisms

Acronyms and initialisms are unique kinds of abbreviations. Acronyms are pronounceable words created from the letters in each word of a term, for example, DARE (Drug Abuse Resistance Education), NASDAQ (National Association of Securities Dealers Automated Quotation), and RAM (Random Access Memory).

Initialisms are created from the letters in each word of a term, but they are spoken as letters since they don't make pronounceable words, for example, AA (Alcoholics Anonymous), AKA (Also Known As), POW (Prisoner Of War), SUV (Sports Utility Vehicle), and FYI (For Your Information).

A pseudo-blend abbreviation is composed of letters that don't allow it to fit as a true acronym or initialism, for example, AWOL (Absent Without Leave) and JPEG (Joint Photographic Experts Group).

The rule for fiction is to use no periods or spaces with abbreviations that include two or more capital letters, which include all acronyms and initialisms.

BEWARE OF RAS SYNDROME

RAS stands for "redundant acronym syndrome," humorously referencing itself as an example of the common mistake people make when they redundantly use a word that's already part of an acronym or initialism. Some examples of this are: CAD design (**C**omputer-**A**ided **D**esign design), GOP party (**G**rand **O**ld **P**arty party), please RSVP (*répondez s'il vous plait* means "please respond" in French, so you're actually saying "please please respond), UPC code (**U**niversal **P**roduct **C**ode code), and VIN number (**V**ehicle **I**dentification **N**umber number).

Abbreviations with Other Punctuation

When an abbreviation that ends with a period falls at the end of a sentence, do not use a second period. If an abbreviation comes inside a sentence, is should be followed by any necessary punctuation.

I live at the very end of Pay Dirt St.
That morning at exactly 7:30 a.m., the band released
their new music video to the world.
John handed me a little blue bag that read Tiffany &
Co.: the famous jewelry store.
The soccer game is at the park at the end of the road—
Harvard St.—after school.

NO PERIODS ALLOWED

A period never accompanies a question mark or an exclamation point, with the exception of an abbreviating period.

Will you meet me at the end of Bliss Ave.?
Why are you still awake? It's 3:42 a.m.!

Pluralizing Abbreviations

To make an abbreviation, acronym, or initialism plural, simply add a lowercase *s*. Do not use an apostrophe.

"How many RSVPs did we get?"
The M.D.s eat in that cafeteria.
The death rate for Soviet POWs held by Germany in
World War II was over 50 percent.
There are so many JPGs on this camera, it's full.

Parentheses and Brackets

When a full sentence is enclosed in parentheses or brackets, the period belongs inside the closing parenthesis or bracket. When the words inside the parenthesis or brackets are part of the surrounding sentence, the period belongs outside.

Michael is a senior (just like Josh Richter). Michael has gotten all straight A's his entire life (just like Josh Richter). Michael will probably go to Yale or Harvard next year (just like Josh Richter).[4]

My daughter was still watching YouTube. (The new laptop she got for Christmas was causing more problems than it was worth.)

The Houston Hawks defeated the Palmer Moose by only 2 [points].

I was running late (couldn't find my keys [or my shoes!]), and my son would be standing outside his school in the rain, waiting.

I went to the grocery store for taco ingredients (ground beef, refried beans, taco seasoning, tortilla shells, cheese, etc.).

5
Question Marks

Most questions are pretty straightforward, but there are some instances when you might wonder if you need a question and, if so, where it should go.

Direct Questions

Use a question mark at the end of a direct question, whether or not the sentence is complete.

"Who let a dog in here?"[1]
Are you going to be home later?
You remembered the cake, didn't you?
I had a question: who took my wallet?
Did you let that cat inside? When you opened the door?

Direct, Unquoted Questions

If you so desire, you can use a question mark at the end of a direct, unquoted question within a sentence.

Is that the one? she wondered.
She would have to ask, Is it mine? when she arrived.
Who did it? is the question.

More Than One Question in a Sentence

Use question marks with a series of questions in the same sentence. In this case, you don't have to capitalize the partial sentences in the list.

Is her office on the first floor? the second? the third?
the fourth?
Who will go with me? will you? or Luke? Kaitlyn?
maybe Grandma?

Declarative and Imperative Sentences

Use a question mark at the end of a declarative or imperative sentence when you want to convey disbelief, sarcasm, surprise, or uncertainty.

You're wearing that?
What are you going to do, fire me?
"You'd blackmail me? Your own cousin?"[2]
Who will care for the widows and orphans?
Amelia Earhart (1897-1939?) was the first female pilot
to fly solo across the Atlantic Ocean.

Use a question mark with a tag question.

A tag question is a small question attached, or tagged, to the end of a sentence. Such questions need a question mark.

It's terribly hot out today, isn't it?
You told him, didn't you?
Wait at the house, will you, until I come back?

Use a question mark to turn a statement into a question.

You can use a question mark at the end of pretty much any sentence to turn it into a question. This is particularly useful when writing dialogue.

You made dinner?
I lost the bracelet?
Marie went to the principal's office?
You saw Doug driving the truck?
Albert forgot your anniversary?

Question Marks with Other Punctuation

A question mark should be placed inside brackets, parentheses, or quotation marks when it's part of the quoted or parenthetical text and outside when it's part of the surrounding sentence.

"Will you please call me Cordelia?" she said eagerly.[3]
The teacher asked, "Do you have the answer?"
What did he mean when he said, "I'm looking for my
    mother"?
I watched through the peep hole (should I open the
    door?) as the man rang the doorbell a second time.
Why make me wear my least favorite color (green)?
"Why would he say, 'You're one of them'?"
Who said, "I write music with an exclamation point!"?

I'd have to ask him—should I?—to know for certain.
How would I manage to . . . ?
"Why did you say that if you . . . ?"

Question Marks in a Title

When a question mark is part of a title, treat it like it's invisible and put any other punctuation marks in the proper places.

In "Who Ya Gonna Call?," the seventh episode of the television show *Psych*, Shawn and Gus help a client who believes he is being haunted.
I always felt bad for Dr. Leo Marvin, the lead character in the movie *What About Bob?*, because he is right to claim that Bob is annoying.
I love the movie *What About Bob?*!
Have you seen the movie *That Thing You Do!*?

Questions That End with an Abbreviation

Use a question mark when a direct question ends with an abbreviation.

Did you remember to shut off all the lights, turn down the heat, lock the door, shut the garage, take out the garbage, etc.?

Question Marks Inside Parentheses

Use a question mark enclosed in parentheses to indicate doubt or uncertainty.

It's an authentic (?) Picasso, or at least it looks like one.
Amelia Earhart died on January 5 (?), 1939.

6
Exclamation Points

Exclamation points are used to indicate yelling, strong emotions, surprise, emphasis, or irony. They also can be used with interjections and direct commands.

Use exclamation points sparingly. If you put them in too often, you'll have no method of distinguishing yelling when you need it. Editors and agents joke that an author is allowed only one exclamation point per manuscript. That's untrue, of course, but they say it to illustrate the importance of not overusing this particular punctuation mark. Its power comes in its rarity.

Also, never use more than one exclamation point in a row.

I never want to see you again!
You took my wallet. Admit it!
Don't touch me!
Look out!

Ouch!
Awesome!
"How amazing is this!"
"You don't want me!" she cried. "You don't want me because I'm not a boy!"[1]

When to Use Multiple Exclamation Points

As with most rules, there are exceptions or reasons why an author might break them. A good reason to use more than one exclamation point is if you want to show the exact wording of a note, email, or text message and the character who wrote it used multiple exclamation points.

come on!! answer me!!!!

Another reason might be if you are writing a novel in a journal style like in this example from *The Princess Diaries* by Meg Cabot.

I can't believe Mr. Gianini told her. I can't believe he told my mother I skipped his stupid review session on Friday!!!![2]

Exclamation Points with other Punctuation

An exclamation point should be placed inside brackets, parentheses, or quotation marks when it's part of the quoted or parenthetical text and outside when it's part of the surrounding sentence.

"Leave!" she yelled.
The police officer screamed, "Get out of the car!"
I can't believe she said that instant coffee tastes "as
    good as Starbucks"!
I walked up to the podium (without tripping!), and the
    dean handed me my diploma.
I can't believe this is happening to me (again)!
Who said, "I write music with an exclamation point!"?
"Oh, sure. You always say, 'It wasn't me'!"
I'll have to go—I can't!—to confront the thief.

Exclamation Points in a Title

When an exclamation point is part of a title, treat it like it's invisible and put any other punctuation marks in the proper places.

In "He Loves Me, He Loves Me Not, He Loves Me,
    Oops He's Dead!," the eleventh episode of the
    television show *Psych*, Shawn and Gus help a client
    who believes he was abducted by aliens.
I love the movie *What About Bob?*!
Have you seen the movie *That Thing You Do!*?
Tom Hanks worked as a director on *That Thing You
    Do!*, *From the Earth to the Moon*, *Band of
    Brothers*, and *Larry Crowne*.

Exclamatory Sentences That End with an Abbreviation

When an exclamatory sentence ends with an abbreviation, you may use an exclamation point along with the period that belongs with the abbreviation.

Mom wants me up and ready by 4:30 a.m.!

7
Commas

Commas are by far the most widely used form of punctuation in fiction. Commas can separate, enclose, introduce, and omit. Of all the punctuation marks, the comma is the one I see misused the most.

Commas and Coordinating Conjunctions

When you use a coordinating conjunction (and, but, for, nor, or, so, yet) to connect two independent clauses (complete sentences), you usually need a comma before the conjunction.

Almost everyone on earth likes chocolate, but I can't live without it.

Coach didn't put me into the game, so I quit the team.

Katie had practiced hard for the band competition, but she didn't want to go.

One after another it shot out four long things, like two arms and two legs, but it was now too dark to tell what they were.[1]

I don't play piano because I'm forced to, but because I
    enjoy it.
Irene sat down in the low chair, and her grandmother
    left her, shutting the door behind her.[2]

When one or both sentences are very short,
you can make an exception and omit the comma.

The bus departed and we were on our way.

When you use a coordinating conjunction
to connect an independent clause with a
dependent clause (also called an incomplete
sentence, since there is no subject), do not use
a comma before the conjunction.

I went to the concert and made three new friends.
I love working my job at the design firm but also really
    look forward to weekends and holidays.
Coach didn't put me into the game and didn't care.
I miss the dummy by a couple of inches and lose what
    little attention I had been commanding.[3]

An exception to this rule can be made when
one side of the sentence is in extreme contrast to
the other. In that case, a comma before the
conjunction is acceptable.

Your success is not due to wisdom, but dumb luck.
She had won first place in the contest, but was upset.

Do not use a comma between two independent clauses. This creates a comma splice (see page 14).

Incorrect: We went to a movie, we ate pizza afterwards.

Correct: We went to a movie. We ate pizza afterwards.

Correct: We went to a movie, and we ate pizza afterwards.

Correct: Whenever we go to a movie, we eat pizza afterwards.

Correct: We went to a movie; we are pizza afterwards.

Never use a comma after a coordinating conjunction, unless setting off parenthetical text.

Incorrect: Almost everyone on earth likes chocolate but, I can't live without it.

Correct: Almost everyone on earth likes chocolate, but I can't live without it.

Correct: I finished the final exam, and, in spite of my fears, I passed.

Correct: Or, if you're really hungry, we can order pizza.

Correct: And Mitty, like the victims in the smallpox hospitals in 1902, had not been vaccinated.[4]

Use a comma after a dependent clause that comes at the beginning of the sentence.

When a dependent (subordinate) clause comes before the independent clause, you need to set it off with a comma. If the dependent clause comes later in the sentence, you do not need a comma.

When I saw what happened to my car, I cried.
Before Kim can start basketball, she needs to get a
    physical exam.
Unless I see better grades from you, you won't be going
    to any parties.

Use commas to enclose parenthetical text, nonessential information, and appositives.

Use commas to offset information that could be left out of the sentence without changing the meaning.

The girls, however, were late.
My party, which was held last Friday, was a lot of fun.
Chris Pine, star of *Star Trek* and *Wonder Woman
    World*, is Robert Pine's son.
Mike's cousin, David, went with him to the concert.

In that last example, the commas tell the reader that Mike has only one cousin and that his name is David. David's name is an appositive set off by commas because it is nonessential information. In the example below, however, the lack of commas tells the reader that Mike has more than one cousin and that David is the cousin who went with him to the concert.

Mike's cousin David went with him to the concert.

When you aren't certain whether to use commas to set off an appositive, ask yourself if the information is essential. If you could remove the phrase from the sentence and it would still make sense, then it's not essential.

Use a comma in a conditional sentence only when the conditional clause comes at the beginning of the sentence.

A conditional sentence discusses a situation and its consequence. Such sentences contain a conditional clause (often called an if-clause), and a consequence. The word *when* can be used instead of *if*. You only need a comma in this type of sentence when the if-clause is at the beginning of the sentence.

If she's quitting, then I'll have to hire a replacement.
I'll have to hire a replacement if she's quitting.
"If you enjoy the little ones so much, you should hope for an Assignment as Nurturer."[5]
When my dad gets off work early, we eat out.
We eat out when my dad gets off work early.
When he wasn't digging up old bones, Archie Brubaker was teaching at universities in the East.[6]

Use a comma after an introductory phrase.

When you start a sentence with an introductory word group, separate it from the rest of the sentence with a comma. The comma can be omitted in a very short sentence (when the introductory phrase is four words or fewer), though some authors choose to use a comma anyway, like in this first example from Lois Lowry's *The Giver*.

At first, he had been only fascinated.[7]
In fact, Julie not only went to the concert, she went
    with Sebastian.
For the fun of it, I must just tell you about his first patient.[8]
After the anthem, the tributes file back into the Training
    Center lobby and onto the elevators.[9]
After delivering all the newspapers, Mike went home.
During the editing phase for her book, Ann nearly gave up.
When Martin was ready to eat, the waiter brought him
    a salad to start with.
In no time we were in a different state.
Hence we lost.

Use a comma between items in a series.

When three or more words, phrases, or clauses are listed in a series, those should be separated by commas. The serial comma (also called the Oxford comma) is the comma that appears before the conjunction at the end of such a list.

Some style guides deem the use of the serial comma optional, and many authors avoid it. *The Chicago Manual of Style* recommends its use, however, and since the CMOS is the industry standard, I use the serial comma.

It's this, that, or the other.
My favorite chips are Doritos, Ruffles, and Cheetos.
He wore a black baseball cap, tight black jeans, and a black T-shirt.[10]
Beth did the dishes, Kurt mowed the lawn, and I vacuumed the living room carpet.
Marcus left the school, crossed the grassy lawn that led to the football field, and took Washington Boulevard all the way to his father's office.
You can choose from going on a hike up the mountain, playing paintball in the field, going on a canoe ride, or swimming in the pool.
I enjoy movies, cooking, and singing.

If the last item in the list is a pair joined by *and*, that pair should still be preceded by a serial comma and a conjunction.

Some great old cartoon characters are Bugs Bunny, Mickey Mouse, Betty Boop, and Tom and Jerry.
My favorite fabrics are the emerald damask, the brown brocade, and the pink and black chiffon.

Another very good reason to get into the habit of using the serial comma in your writing is that sometimes, when you leave it out, you might accidentally create some confusing or amusing statements. Compare the following sentences:

For the party, we invited the teachers, Melinda, and Gary.
For the party, we invited the teachers, Melinda and Gary.
For the party, we invited the teachers: Melinda and Gary.

If Melinda and Gary aren't teachers but some other profession, the first example sentence is correct. If, however, Melinda and Gary were the only two teachers invited to the party, the second and third examples are correct. The use of the colon in the third sentence leaves no room for confusion whatsoever. Let's try another one.

Restroom use is for the children, disabled and pregnant.
Restroom use is for children and people who are
    disabled or pregnant.

In the first example, only disabled or pregnant children are allowed to use the restroom, which probably isn't the meaning anyone had in mind for that sentence. Rewriting the sentence, as in the second example, clears up the confusion. And how about this sentence?

Pete likes cooking, his family and his friends.
Pete likes cooking, his family, and his friends.

In the first example, Pete has a terrifying interest in cooking his family and friends. In the second example, the serial comma saves the day, making it clear that Pete likes cooking. He likes his family. And he likes his friends.

Use parallel construction when joining similar parts of sentences.

When you write sentences with lists, try to keep the same grammatical structure in each.

Incorrect: Kate purchased <u>a dress</u>, <u>necklace</u>, and <u>a pair of shoes</u> for the wedding.
Correct: Kate purchased <u>a dress</u>, <u>a necklace</u>, and <u>a pair of shoes</u> for the wedding.

Incorrect: Jeremy hates <u>writing</u>, <u>to read</u>, and <u>football</u>.
Correct: Jeremy hates <u>to write</u>, <u>to read</u>, and <u>to play football</u>.
Correct: Jeremy hates <u>writing</u>, <u>reading</u>, and <u>playing football</u>.

Incorrect: Michelle wants <u>a cat</u>, <u>to visit Paris</u>, <u>the second season of *Stranger Things* on DVD</u>, and <u>for her dad to come visit</u> for her birthday.
Correct: For her birthday, Michelle wants <u>a cat</u>, <u>a trip to Paris</u>, <u>a DVD of the second season of *Stranger Things*</u>, and <u>a visit from her dad</u>.

Use a comma between coordinate adjectives, not between cumulative adjectives.

Adjectives are coordinate if they can be joined with the word *and* or if they can be scrambled and still make sense. Commas are required between coordinate adjectives. Consider the following sentence:

Michael is a strong, tall, talented basketball player.

First, let's replace the commas with the word *and* to see if the meaning stays the same.

Michael is a strong and tall and talented basketball player.

That works. Our next test is to scramble the adjectives to see if that has an effect.

Michael is a talented, strong, tall basketball player.

The sentence still has the same meaning. So we know the sentence works with commas.

Cumulative adjectives, on the other hand, lean on one another with each one modifying a larger word group. They do not require commas in between. Consider this sentence:

Four small white doves flew toward me.

When we test this sentence by putting the word *and* between the adjectives, it doesn't make sense.

Four and small and white doves flew toward me.

Scrambling the adjectives also changes the meaning of the sentence.

White small four doves flew toward me.

So we know these are cumulative adjectives and require no commas between them.

Use a comma after an interjection.

This is a rule I never forgot because of the old *Schoolhouse Rock!* cartoons. Those catchy tunes with delightful animation made learning punctuation and grammar fun. If you ever have time, look up *Schoolhouse Rock!* on YouTube. They're great.

One song in particular taught me that interjections were set apart from a sentence by an exclamation point or by a comma if the feeling just wasn't as strong. I never forgot it.

You can also set off interjections with a period, if you want to convey something more serious or final.

"Gee, do I have to?"
"Oh, *no*," Mother murmured sympathetically.[11]
"Oh, yes! Can I really?"
"Oh! Why did you do that?"
"Yes! I've been dying for you to ask."
No. This was not happening.
"Hey, are you coming or not?"
"Ouch! That hurt!"
Well, I guess I didn't get the job.
"Yay!"

"Aww, it's so cute!"
"Why did you do that when I—*blast!* This is terrible!"
"Rats." And Charlie Brown walked home alone.

Use commas to separate a name or title used in direct address.

I went over this when I talked about common mistakes I see in manuscripts (see page 13). To review, when a speaker uses the name or title of the person or group to whom he is talking, set off that name or title with commas.

"Mom, can you come here a minute?"
"I'm not listening to you anymore, Paul."
"Aye, Captain. I'm on it."
"All right, guys, this is it. Make or break."[12]
"Come with me, children."
"I will do so at once, Your Highness."

Use commas to set apart quoted material or dialogue.

Nothing marks a beginning writer faster than mistakes in punctuating dialogue. It can be tricky to figure out how to do this right, but once you learn, you'll never forget. See Chapter 14 for the rules on punctuating dialogue.

Commas and the word *Too*

When the word *too* is used to mean *also* at the end of a sentence, setting it off with commas is optional. Only use commas with the word *too* if you want to add a pause to create emphasis or to signify an abrupt change in thought.

I want to come too.
I too want to come.
I like anchovies, too.
I, too, like anchovies.
Keri wasn't sure she wanted to break up, but she knew, too, that she wasn't ready to get married, either.

Other Places to Use Commas

Use a comma every three decimal places for numbers higher than 999.

We counted 1,623 ballots.
I am 18,495 days old.

When writing out the date, separate the day and year numbers with a comma.

I was born on December 12, 1982, in Maine.

Use a comma between a city and state.

I was born in August, Maine.

8
Colons

A colon means *as follows*. It's used to introduce something (or a series of things).

Use a colon after a complete sentence to direct attention to a list.

When you have a list to share, using a colon is a great way to announce that list.

Give us the following construction materials: wood, hammers, and nails.
This summer our family plans to visit four western states: Arizona, Utah, Colorado, and New Mexico.

A colon should not divide noun from verb or preposition from its object.

Incorrect: The materials I need to build are: wood, hammers, and nails.
Incorrect: Our family plans to go to: Arizona, Utah, and Colorado.

Note that these sentences would be correct if you were to drop the colon.

Correct: The materials I need to build are wood, hammers, and nails.
Correct: Our family plans to go to Arizona, Utah, and Colorado.

An exception to the rule of not allowing a colon to separate a noun from its verb or a preposition from its object *and* the rule of only using a colon at the end of a complete sentence is to add *as follows* or *the following* after your sentence fragment.

Marcia's daily workout was supposed to include at least the following: twenty sit-ups, ten push-ups, and fifteen minutes of cardio.
The reasons she moved from the country to the city were as follows: public transportation, housing options, and jobs.

Use a colon at the end of a complete sentence to direct attention to an appositive.

An appositive is a word or phrase that means the same thing as the word or phrase beside it. Be sure to place the colon right beside the word(s) you're redefining.

We found the cat sleeping in her favorite <u>spot:</u> the tree in the backyard.
Before graduation, I must conquer <u>one obstacle:</u> passing all my classes.

Shelby was shocked at <u>what she saw:</u> her reflection.

The Dursleys' house had <u>four bedrooms:</u> one for Uncle Vernon and Aunt Petunia, one for visitors (usually Uncle Vernon's sister, Marge), one where Dudley slept, and one where Dudley kept all the toys and things that wouldn't fit into his first bedroom. [1]

Use a colon after a complete sentence to direct attention to a quotation.

This is a nice way of setting up a quotation to pack a punch in your writing.

Consider the words of Mother Theresa: "Even the rich are hungry for love, for being cared for, for being wanted, for having someone to call their own."

And she put her small hand upon his and a little scuffle ensued, Tom pretending to resist in earnest but letting his hand slip by degrees till these words were revealed: *"I love you."* [2]

Capitalization and the Colon

How do you know whether or not to capitalize the first word following a colon? Always have the word be lowercase except in the following circumstances.

1. If the first word is a proper noun.

The people who should be on the bus are the following: <u>Mark</u>, Christa, Drew, and Kelley.

Our book tour would take us to five major cities: <u>Nashville</u>, Atlanta, St. Louis, Houston, and Phoenix.

2. If the colon precedes a definition or a direct quotation.

When Christy got angry at Karen, Jill told her not to "Jake Out": <u>An act of turning into a werewolf, inspired by the book *Twilight*.</u>

The poignant words of Douglas Adams state: <u>"Flying is learning how to throw yourself at the ground and miss."</u>

3. If the colon comes before two or more related sentences.

Robert had three options: <u>He could walk the six miles to the library. He could call someone and beg a ride. Or he could just take Grandma Nan's car.</u>

4. If the colon introduces dialogue lines in a speech or drama.

Juliette: <u>Then, window, let day in, and let life out.</u>
Romeo: <u>Farewell, farewell! One kiss and I'll descend.</u>

5. If the colon is used in a book title to separate the title from the subtitle.

In 2013, Stephanie Morrill and Jill Williamson collaborated to write the book *Go Teen Writers<u>:</u> How to Turn a First Draft into a Published Book.*
Gary Chapman's *The 5 Love Languages<u>:</u> The Secret to Love That Lasts* has transformed millions of relationships.

Use a colon in the salutation of a business letter.

There is little reason to use this rule when writing fiction, but there is always the chance you might want to show a full letter in your manuscript. And if that letter is a business letter, you'll want to format it correctly. You can find lots of examples how to format a business letter online.

Use a colon to separate hours from minutes when using numerals to write the time.

The time of death was 2:14 this afternoon.

Use a colon when writing ratios.

They have a 1:8 chance of winning the relay race.

9
Semicolons

Some editors and authors frown on using semicolons in fiction. Semicolons are a legitimate form of punctuation, however, and it's your right as a novelist to use them. If you so insist, do so sparingly.

Capitalization and the Semicolon

The first word after a semicolon should always be lowercase.

Semicolons and Independent Clauses

A semicolon is used to separate closely related independent clauses not joined by a coordinating conjunction. In other words, use a semicolon if you want to glue together two complete sentences that are similar in subject.

They did this when they were angry; speaking by way of text messages kept the screaming to all caps.[1]

Martin Luther King, Jr. said that "Hate begets hate; violence begets violence; toughness begets a greater toughness."

Ten finalists performed to be the next American Idol; only two finalists remain.

Mr. Sanchez is a successful chef; however, he won't eat his own cooking.

Rules for This Rule

An independent clause is a set of words that creates a complete sentence. If you are using a semicolon to join two clauses together and one of those clauses isn't an independent clause, a semicolon is the wrong choice and you should use a comma instead.

Also, it is incorrect to use a semicolon if you have a coordinating conjunction (and, but, or, etc.) between your two clauses.

If you put a comma between two independent clauses, you will create a comma splice, an error I talked about in the chapter on common mistakes (see page 14).

Use a semicolon with conjunctive adverbs.

Conjunctive adverbs (also, besides, finally, however, in contrast, instead, otherwise, then, therefore, etc.) connect words, phrases, and clauses to give clarity to a sentence. Conjunctive adverbs behave like coordinating conjunctions because they connect two main clauses; however, when you connect two independent clauses with a conjunctive adverb, you need a semicolon, not a comma.

Micah could have told the truth; instead, he told several lies.
Gina shopped all day; however, she didn't buy anything.
Isaac is an introvert; in contrast, his brother is outgoing.

Semicolons Between Items in a Series

A semicolon is also used between items in a series that contain internal punctuation.

That means, you're already listing things, but then you list something with commas, which messes up your list. You need to somehow set apart any commas that are serving a different purpose. You do this by using semicolons to separate the main items in your list. That frees you up to use commas inside the semicolons, if needed.

I ate berries; toast; eggs scrambled with sausage, tomatoes, hash browns, and cheese; and a smoothie for breakfast.

Some popular fantasy novels for teens are *Harry Potter*, starring the boy wizard with a lightning-bolt scar; *Eragon*, where a young boy becomes a dragon rider; and the timeless *Chronicles of Narnia*, in which a group of children enter a magical land through a wardrobe.

10
Dashes

There are two kinds of dashes that are used most often in writing. The em dash — is the longest one, and the en dash – is just a bit shorter. These are both different from a hyphen - which is the shortest of them all.

Please note, my instructions for creating dashes is for the word processing program Microsoft Word. This doesn't work online. If you're online, you can either use two hyphens in a row for an em dash or copy-and-paste one from your word processing program.

The Em Dash

The em dash is used to show all kinds of interruptions in speech, thought, or narrative. It can also be used to emphasize, show a change in thought, or set words apart from others.

To create the em dash, type a word, then type two hyphens, then type the next word, then type a space. Do not put any spaces until you are done with the sequence. What you type will look like this: word--word(space)

When you hit that last space bar, the two dashes will convert to an em dash. It's pretty cool. If you can't figure out how to make that super long em dash show up, it's acceptable to use two hyphens in place of the em dash--like that.

I often hear confusion over how J. K. Rowling used spaces with the em dashes in her *Harry Potter* books. Here is an example:

Incorrect in the USA: Seamus got so impatient that he prodded it with his wand and set fire to it — Harry had to put it out with his hat.[1]

J. K. Rowling is British, so she follows British style punctuation rules. If you're writing novels in, or wish to publish books in, the United States of America, follow the rules in *The Chicago Manual of Style*. That means no space before or after an em dash.

Use an em dash to signify an interruption.

Interruptions can come in narrative.

Armed with a one-sheet, a stack of business cards, and a perfect logline—nothing would keep Katie from pitching her novel.

When an interruption comes in dialogue, it's not necessary to use a said tag to tell the reader that the speaker interrupted. Instead, use the em dash to show the interruption.

"I don't know why all of this happened to me," Julie said. "Maybe it's because—"
"I don't want to hear your excuses, Jules. I'm sick of them!"

Use an em dash to signify a break in thought.

Breaks in thought or dialogue are natural, so using em dashes to show breaks can make your dialogue and narrative sound realistic.

"I can't believe Mr. Thomas ate all my—did you just say Kate wrecked the car?"
"Your, your, your, ba—Mary, you on the nest?"[2]

Use em dashes to set off parenthetical material you want to emphasize.

If you'd like to call attention to or emphasize certain words within a sentence, an em dash is an effective way to accomplish that.

The other day—Thursday, to be more exact—Dr.
    Mortimer lunched with us.[3]
Everything that went wrong—from the C- on our
    history project to Tom breaking up with her—Shelly
    blamed on me.
Can you believe that Susie Walker—a cheerleader and a
    freshman—won homecoming queen?

Use an em dash to set off an introductory noun or pronoun with an appositive.

To emphasize an appositive, you can use an em dash as long as it comes directly after the noun or pronoun it's describing.

Threats—that was the approach John's father used to
    get his children to obey.
A must for the male hipster—beard, skinny jeans,
    glasses, and ankle boots.
Embarrassment, loss of trust, and shame—such were
    the consequences of getting caught in a lie.

Use an em dash to set off appositives that contain commas.

If your appositive is extra-long and complicated and contains many commas, an em dash can be used to set it off.

When you apply your make-up—foundation, eyeliner, mascara, eye shadow, blush, and lipstick—be sure to follow the consumer guidelines.

Em Dashes with Other Punctuation

You can use an em dash with an abbreviating period, an exclamation point, or a question mark, but not with a comma, a colon, or a semicolon.

I wish I could have gone to the show—if only!—then I
    could have met the actor too.
The alarm went off super early—three a.m.—and it
    scared me to death!
I wanted to go—did I dare ask for more time off?—
    because if I didn't, I knew that Marcus would.

The En Dash

An en dash is pretty much used exclusively with numbers, so it's not a tool you will need very often in writing fiction.

To create the en dash, type a word, type a space, then type one hyphen, then type the next word, then type a space. What you type will look like this: word(space)-word(space)

When you hit that last space bar, the dash will convert to an en dash.

You'll have to go back and take out the first space once the dash is converted. It's proper format that no space appear before or after the en dash.

Use an en dash to connect inclusive numbers: page numbers, dates, or Bible references.

In this instance, the en dash means "up to and including" or "through."

Please read in your text pages 86–92.
I went to college from 1993–1997.
I read John 3:16–17 and it changed my life.

The 2-Em Dash

A 2-em dash is created by putting two em dashes side by side with no space between.

Use a 2-em dash to omit a missing word or part of a word, to conceal a name, to block out an expletive, or to show missing or illegible words from quoted material.

When the whole word is missing, put a space on both sides of the 2-em dash. When part of the word is missing, there should be no space between the existing part of the word and the 2-em dash.

This isn't a very commonly used form of punctuation, especially for fiction. I included it because I thought it might be fun for those of you who write mystery or suspense.

Mr. T—— and Mrs. S—— were secretly married.
What the —— is going on here?
The car was purchased by a Mr. B——min [Benjamin?]
    Walsh.

11
Ellipses

Ellipses are used to show a long pause, confusion, faltering, trailing off, passing out, and words that grow too soft to hear. They're also used at the end of a deliberately unfinished sentence and to show an omission of words.

Allow me to clear up how this word is spelled and pronounced, both in the singular and plural. The singular word is ellipsis [ih-lip-sis], and the plural is ellipses [ih-lip-seez].

To create an ellipsis, type three periods in a row and hit enter. Most word processing programs will automatically format those three periods into a preformatted ellipsis. If your program does not, you can simply type three periods in a row ... or you can type three periods with a space in between each . . . The latter is what my publishers wanted, however, every publisher has their own guidelines and will let you know their preference during the editing stage. You won't get rejected for putting a space between the periods or leaving them out. Just be consistent.

Indie authors creating their own ebooks should use preformatted ellipses ... so they won't get split at the end of a line:

"I see the Stone . . . I'm presenting it to my master . . . but where is it?"[1]

There should also be a space before and after each ellipsis, unless it falls at the beginning or end of a quoted sentence. In that case, no space should come between the ellipsis and the quotation marks.

Incorrect: "Can you. . .believe it?"
Correct: "Can you . . . believe it?"

Incorrect: " . . . But he said that I . . . "
Correct: "But how will I . . ."
Correct: ". . . because I said so."

Use ellipses to show hesitation.

Ellipses can be used to show thought or dialogue that falters or trails off. If your character is confused, insecure, uncertain, falling asleep, or passing out, an ellipsis is the tool to use to convey this.

"Where . . . I had it right . . . the medallion . . . I must have dropped it!"
"I want to go there . . . first thing . . . in the morning."
"Okay. I'll tell you who shot me. It was . . ." Kit's body went limp in John's arms.
"I see the Stone . . . I'm presenting it to my master . . . but where is it?"[1]

Use an ellipsis to leave something purposely unsaid.

Sometimes you might deliberately leave a sentence unfinished, perhaps to insinuate something, to make a point, or because you only need to say part of the sentence to make yourself clear. An ellipsis can communicate to readers that there are words left unsaid.

And they sang that old song. You know. The one that
    goes "Should auld acquaintance be forgot . . ."
"Carol promised to come tonight, but . . ."

Use an ellipsis to show omitted words.

An ellipsis can also be used to show an omission of words. If you want to shorten or remove part of a quotation, use an ellipsis in place of any omitted words—as long as you are careful to retain the author's original meaning.

Let's look at this writing quotation from Gore Vidal.

> Each writer is born with a repertory company in his head. Shakespeare has perhaps 20 players, and Tennessee Williams has about 5, and Samuel Beckett one—and maybe a clone of that one. I have 10 or so, and that's a lot. As you get older, you become more skillful at casting them.

By using an ellipsis, I could shorten the quotation. In the following example, I used a pre-formatted ellipses so you could tell the ellipses apart from the period.

"Each writer is born with a repertory company in his head. ... As you get older, you become more skillful at casting them."

Another type of omission of words would be the silence when someone is on a phone call and the other characters in the room cannot hear what the absent person is saying.

"Hello? . . . Where are you? . . . I see . . . No, we can't come right now. We're waiting for Albert, then we'll leave . . . Okay, good-bye."

Or consider this example from John Grisham's *The Firm* where the character Ray is eavesdropping on a woman and only catching snippets of a conversation.

The blonde took a phone on the end and turned her back to him. She spoke softly. He could hear only pieces.
". . . checked in . . . Room 622 . . . Mobile . . . some help . . . I can't . . . an hour? . . . yes . . . hurry . . ."[2]

The Mythical Four-Dot Ellipsis
I have seen in some novels what looks like a four-dot ellipsis at the end of a sentence or paragraph.

There is no such thing as a four-dot ellipsis.

In this section I will again use the preformatted ellipses so that you can differentiate the ellipses from the periods.

There are two reasons to have four periods in a row. First, if you want to imply an omission of one or more thoughts after a complete sentence in order to create a dramatic pause, you could put an ellipsis between two sentences.

Joshua fell off the cliff. ... He was gone.

Second, you will have four periods in a row when you omit part of a quotation or passage, as I had at the top of page 63 when I shortened Gore Vidal's quotation. This happens either by taking out one or more complete sentences or by taking out the beginning of a sentence. In both cases you would have one period at the end of the sentence before the omitted material, then three periods for the ellipsis. Consider the following examples. The first quotation was said by Chief Joseph of the Nez Perce, the second, by President Ronald Reagan.

"Tell General Howard I know his heart. What he told me before, I have it in my heart. I am tired of fighting. ... The old men are all dead."

"We've grown used to wonders in this century. It's hard to dazzle us. ... the United States space program has been doing just that."

12
Hyphens

A hyphen is used to join two or more words to create a compound word. It is also used at the end of a line in a book to divide a word that was too long to fit.

It's not always easy to know whether to hyphenate a compound word. I decide in one of two ways. I look up the word in *Merriam-Webster's New Collegiate Dictionary*, or I make the choice to leave out the hyphen.

A good example of the latter is how I spell the word *fairytale*. When I look it up in *Merriam-Webster's*, it is spelled *fairy-tale*. Since I'm a speculative fiction author, I've given myself permission to spell it without the hyphen. The same is true of the word *storyworld*. No version of this word appears in *Merriam-Webster's*, therefore the proper way to spell it would be as an open compound of two separate words: **story world**. Due to my profession, however, I've coined it in a closed compound form.

I've given myself permission to break those rules due to my experience as a professional author. Also, if you read fantasy or science fiction, it's common to see authors creating their own compound words for fantasy terms, be they hyphenated or not. This is perfectly acceptable.

This does not, however, give you permission to freely misspell any compound word you feel like misspelling. There is no reason to spell **rainbow**, **basketball**, **fireworks**, or **airplane** like **rain bow**, **basket ball**, **fire works**, or **air plane**, nor is it correct to spell them **rain-bow**, **basket-ball**, **fire-works**, or **air-plane**—unless the word falls at the end of a line as basketball did a few lines above. So if you're not sure, grab that dictionary and double check.

Hyphens with Compound Adjectives

A compound adjective is two or more words joined together to modify the same noun. Compound adjectives are read as a single word, and they should only be hyphenated when they come *before* the noun they modify.

So they took him and laid him out of the way on the
    <u>drawing-room sofa</u> with a drink at his elbow, and
    they went back to their dark business.[1]
It was a tiny, <u>grubby-looking pub</u>.[2]
He was around 5'10" with a muscular neck and a
    <u>don't-mess-with-me body</u>.[3]
The werewolf was a <u>cold-blooded killer</u>.
I've never met a more <u>close-minded man</u>.
I can't believe she read the entire <u>650-page book</u>.
When I read the <u>back-cover copy</u>, I was hooked.
The Grant family adopted a <u>two-year-old girl</u> from Africa.

What if the compound adjective comes after the noun it modifies? In that case, it is not usually hyphenated.

By nature, <u>Jamie</u> is <u>easy going</u>, which sometimes gets her into trouble.

Since "easy going" comes after the noun it is modifying, "Jamie", it is not hyphenated. But if "easy-going" came before the word it is modifying, "nature", it would be hyphenated.

Jamie's <u>easy-going nature</u> sometimes gets her into
    trouble.

Here are some more examples of compound adjectives that are not hyphenated.

Michael and Dave's <u>apartment</u> is <u>off campus</u>.
The <u>job</u> was going to be <u>long term</u>.
That <u>burner</u> is <u>red hot</u>.
<u>Sophie</u> is <u>well respected</u> in the art community.

The <u>manuscript</u> is now <u>up to date</u>.
The Grant family adopted <u>a girl</u> from Africa who is <u>two years old</u>.

Some compound adjectives are always hyphenated, like any combination of *in-law*. When in doubt, consult a dictionary.

She is my mother-in-law.
The school's computer system is state-of-the-art.

Compounds with Verb and Noun Forms

Some compounds have a verb form and a noun form. They should be separate words when used as verbs and one word when used as nouns.

I can't believe the computer <u>shut down</u>. (verb)
Can you believe the computer suffered a <u>shutdown</u>? (noun)

Do not hyphenate compounds formed with -ly adverbs.

There is no need to put a hyphen after an -ly adverb since such words modify a modifier, not a noun.

She had perfectly coiffed hair.
Ancient Greek was a wholly irrelevant college course.

Add a hyphen for clarity.

Sometimes what you've written is grammatically correct but confusing. In such cases, adding a hyphen will provide clarity.

Mark loved the red trimmed black Corvette.
Mark loved the red-trimmed black Corvette.
Mark loved the red trimmed-black Corvette.

The first sentence is unclear due to the lack of hyphens or even a comma to help the reader discern the meaning. The second sentence tells us that the Corvette is black with red trim. The third sentence tells us the Corvette is red with black trim.

Be careful where you put the hyphen.

It can be easy to confuse readers by accidentally putting your hyphen in the wrong place. Make sure your hyphen is doing exactly what you want it to do.

At the zoo, Kylie saw a man-eating bear.
At the zoo, Kylie saw a man eating bear.

In the first sentence, Kylie saw a bear that is known for eating humans. In the second sentence, Kylie saw a man eating a bear. Eww.

Bo walked through the heavy metal-detector at the airport.
Bo walked through the heavy-metal detector at the airport.

In the first sentence, Bo walked through a metal detector that weighted a lot. In the second sentence, it sounds like he walked through a detector of heavy-metal music.

Use suspended hyphens to simplify adjectives.

When you are listing two or more of the same type of compound, you can omit the second part of the compound and replace it with a space or comma—in all but the final compound in the list.

We are shopping for a three- or four-bedroom house.
Submit a one- to two-page synopsis.
Five-, six-, seven-, and eight-year-old children meet in the blue classroom.
Yankee- and Mets-obsessed fans don't always get along.
The sky was mottled with small clouds. The sun was not yet up, but some of their fluffy edges had caught his light, and hung out orange- and gold-coloured fringes upon the air.[4]

Use a hyphen with words that are meant to be read as a single word.

Some words are meant to be read as one word and should be hyphenated.

We got stopped at the US-Canada border.

Use a hyphen with fractions that are modifiers.

If you're writing a fraction as an adjective or adverb, use a hyphen. If your fraction is a noun, it should not be hyphenated.

My one-fourth slice of the cake was huge. (adjective)
Melanie gave me one fourth of her cake. (noun)

Use a hyphen when writing out numbers twenty-one through ninety-nine, even when those numbers are part of larger numbers.

There were sixty-three people at the party.
The total votes counted came to three hundred and forty-two.

Use a hyphen when joining a number or letter to a word. Notice that the single letter is capitalized and is not part of an abbreviation.

He wore a blue T-shirt.
In the middle of the road, Mike did a U-turn.
"I will not watch that X-rated movie."
They live in the A-frame house at the end of the street.
Shelby ran the 100-meter dash.
It's a three-mile hike to the store.
I bought a fifty-cent stamp.
Jane is part of a 250-year legacy.

Using Hyphens with Prefixes

It's tricky to know whether or not to use a hyphen with a prefix. Sometimes you do, and sometimes you don't. Use a dictionary to check if you're not sure.

My ex-husband is in prison.
I am a self-made man.
Billy Joel sang about an uptown girl.
I co-own that company.
We divorced but still manage to coexist peaceably.
We saw an off-Broadway show.
That offbeat music is driving me nuts.
Did you preview that movie too?
It's a pre-war era gun.
Did you pick up the antibiotics for the baby?
Captain Jack Sparrow is a famous anti-hero.

You always use a hyphen, however, when joining a prefix to a proper noun (a capitalized word) or a date.

You are totally un-American.
That gown is pre-Georgian.
In Jerry Spinelli's *Stargirl*, nearly the entire school participated in an anti-Stargirl shunning.
By the mid-1960s, NASA was well into the race to put a man on the moon.
We boarded the trans-American flight.
I don't vacation until the post-game season.
Pre-1990, few people owned cell phones.

13
Quotation Marks

Quotation marks—also called quotes, quote marks, or speech marks—are primarily used to enclose direct quotations, speech, or dialogue. When reading pre-published manuscripts, I see so many mistakes with punctuating dialogue tags that I dedicated the entire next chapter to that subject alone.

There are two types of quotation marks. Double quotation marks " " have two marks on each side of the quoted material. Single quotation marks ' ' have a single mark on each side of the quoted material.

The only reason to ever use single quotation marks is when you need to quote something that is already inside double quotation marks.

Use quotation marks around dialogue, quotations, and quoted words.

Quotation marks are used to set apart dialogue and quotations or quoted material that is no longer than a few sentences—the actual rules are about 100 words long or four lines or fewer. Anything longer should be set apart as a block quotation.

"Can you believe it?" Mary asked.
Only Achan uses the oath "Pig snout."
As Shakespeare said, "To thine own self be true."
One of my favorite bits of writing advice is how Michael Crichton said "Books aren't written—they're rewritten. Including your own. It is one of the hardest things to accept, especially after the seventh rewrite hasn't quite done it."
Alexander Pope's poem "An Essay on Criticism" does *not* begin with his famous line "To err is human, to forgive divine."

Do not use quotation marks with a block quotation.

Block quotations are used for long passages. Cite the source in the introductory paragraph, set apart the quotation by inserting a blank line before and after, then indent the right and left margins.

We learned how Thomas Jefferson wrote the first draft of the *Declaration of Independence*, then Mr. Arthur made us memorize the first paragraph.

When in the Course of human events it becomes necessary for one people to dissolve the political bands which have connected them with another and to assume among the powers of the earth, the separate and equal station to which the Laws of Nature and of Nature's God entitle them, a decent respect to the opinions of mankind requires that they should declare the causes which impel them to the separation.

Do not use quotation marks with indirect quotations.

If the words you are quoting aren't verbatim, then you don't need to use quotation marks.

Michael Crichton said that rewriting books is one of the hardest things to accept, especially after the seventh rewrite.

Use single quotation marks only when marking a quotation within a quotation.

"An Alpha victory all around," Mr. S said. "But 'It is the fight alone that pleases us, not the victory.' Blaise Pascal."

"And I would like to add," Isaac said, "that 'A date without a goodnight kiss is like a doughnut without frosting.' And that quote is *all* me."[1]

Use quotation marks when quoting a definition or the text on a label or sign.

A martinet is not a stringed puppet. *Merriam-Webster's* defines it as "a strict disciplinarian." The label on the bottle read "poison."

Quotation Marks with Other Punctuation

Quotation marks always come after a comma, period, question mark, or exclamation point.

"I am so hungry," Mark said.
Shelly opened the door. "Hello, Dad."
"Afraid you're going to be late?"[2]
They sang in unison: "Starboy!"[3]
"Can you believe that Doug said, 'It is the west, and Juliet is the moon,' when he was supposed to say, 'It is the east, and Juliet is the sun?'"

Exceptions

When a question mark or exclamation point is part of a quotation, it should go inside the end quotes.

"But at least he said, 'See, how she leans her cheek upon her hand!' the right way."

But when a question mark or exclamation point is not part of a quotation but part of the speaker's dialogue, it goes outside the quotation.

"I can't believe he said, 'You can't act'!"

Where to Put the Colon or Semicolon

Unlike periods and commas, when a colon or semicolon is part of the sentence, they are never put inside the quotation.

The bumper sticker read "My other car is a TARDIS": a spaceship that looks like a telephone box.
I love the song "Call Me Maybe"; my boyfriend hates it.

Should you use a space between side-by-side single and double quotation marks?

When a double quotation mark and a single quotation mark are side by side, publishers sometimes put a space between them. You can put a space if you'd like, or you can put them right next to one another. Whatever you decide, be consistent throughout your manuscript. Also, always make sure your quotation marks are pointing the correct direction.

" 'Genius not only diagnoses the situation but supplies the answers,' so said Robert Graves," Mr. S said.[4]

Use quotation marks to denote that a word or expression is unusual, special, ironic, or sarcastic.

He did some "experimenting" in his college days.
Jane's "special" hairbrush came from a pet store.
I just "love" cat hair all over my clothes.

Use quotation marks when writing about a specific word.

Julian uses the word "hate" at least once an hour.
"What does 'panache' mean again?" she asked.

Do not use quotation marks to emphasize a word or phrase.

Emphasizing a word is different than marking it as special or specific. When you want to emphasize a word or phrase, use italics, not quotation marks (see page 96).

Use quotation marks around the titles of songs, articles, and poems.

The music video for "Roundtable Rival" is so much fun.
I sold an article called "Is He the One?"
I memorized the poem "Sick" by Shel Silverstein.

Quoting Song Lyrics in a Novel

Lyrics are intellectual property, owned by music companies that are pretty aggressive in protecting their rights. Unfortunately, fair use law doesn't usually apply with lyrics, as the music industry seems to want permission for the use of even one line. This means you need to pay to quote a song in your book.

My advice has always been don't bother, but if you're set on it and willing to pay, Google "quoting songs in a novel" for more information.

"What?" he asked.

14
Dialogue Tags

When I look back at some of my first manuscripts, guess what I see? Lots of mistakes in punctuating my dialogue!

I share that so that you can understand that many authors struggle in this area. The good news is, like all punctuation rules, you can learn these too.

So, if you're not sure when to use a comma or period, where to put the quotation marks, or how to use an ellipsis with your character's dialogue, read on.

There are three types of dialogue tags used in fiction: said tags, action tags, and narrative or thought tags. The word *tag* simply means that you're adding extra information to a sentence as a way to label the dialogue so that the reader knows who said it.

Start a new paragraph each time you have a new speaker or new character's action.

Keep a character's actions and dialogue in the same paragraph. If a new character speaks or acts, start a new paragraph.

The following example is confusing because there are paragraphs that have more than one character speaking. Don't do this!

> Logan yelled out Zaq's open door. "Check under the hood, Eli." Eli gestured to the van. "The doors are locked!" He could pop the hood if he got on the ground under the engine, but he'd need a long screwdriver, and Riggs didn't have any tools. "Do you have a spare key?" Riggs asked.
>
> "No. And I'm not going to break a window, either, Logan, so don't suggest it." Logan said, "If you did break a window, I could hotwire it."

To fix this, we would start a new paragraph for each character's speech and/or actions.

> Logan yelled out Zaq's open door. "Check under the hood, Eli."
>
> Eli gestured to the van. "The doors are locked!" He could pop the hood if he got on the ground under the engine, but he'd need a long screwdriver. And Riggs didn't have any tools.
>
> "Do you have a spare key?" Riggs asked.
>
> "No. And I'm not going to break a window, either, Logan, so don't suggest it," Eli said.
>
> "If you did break a window, I could hotwire it," Logan said.[1]

Punctuating Dialogue That is Part of the Surrounding Sentence

There are some instances when the dialogue or quotation requires no tag because it is part of the surrounding sentence.

When the audience finally settles down, he [Peeta] finally chokes out a quiet "Thank you" and returns to his seat.[2]
Mark said that his suit was "not the nicest one on the dance floor."

Punctuating Said Tags

A said tag assigns the dialogue to a speaker by using the word "said" or a variation of that word (asked, yelled, whispered, etc.). A said tag is connected to the dialogue with a comma, unless the dialogue is a question or requires an exclamation point. When using a said tag, the pronoun must be lowercase unless you are using a proper name. Pay attention to the underlined parts of the examples below for proper punctuation.

"I'm sorry," the girl said.
"I did," his father said, laughing.[3]
"I do," Father said.
"I am the President of the United States," Abraham said.
"What do you want?" she asked.
"Since when is cutting class a national emergency?" Derek asked.[4]
"Leave me alone!" he screamed.
"Leave me alone!" Mike screamed.
"I can't believe I'm telling you this," Mindy said, "but I'm one of them."

In that last example, the said tag divided the sentence, so a comma was used on both sides of the said tag. If you do this, make sure the division falls in a natural place for your character to pause. Read the dialogue out loud to see what sounds best.

Another way to write that same sentence would be to divide it into two sentences.

"I can't believe I'm telling you this," Mindy said. "I'm one of them."

You could also combine action with your said tag.

Mindy took a deep breath and said, "I can't believe I'm telling you this, but I'm one of them."

Punctuating Action and Thought Tags

Action and thought tags are complete sentences that identify the speaker by what they are doing, thinking, or describing. Because we see a character act or think in the same paragraph as dialogue, we know that person is the one speaking.

Since action tags and thought tags are sentences, they are punctuated like sentences.

Action tag: Krista rolled her eyes. "What do you want, Paul?"

Action tag: "Get out!" Beth slammed the door in her mother's face.

Thought tag: "You called them, didn't you?" I was so mad, I could hardly even see straight. "You called and told them we were coming here."[5]

Thought tag: "Don't worry about it." But I don't think I meant it.

Thought and action tag: This reminded me of a nightmare I'd had when I was a little kid. I put on a brave face. "I'll go."

Action tag: "If you want to come, get in." Kyle opened the car door. "Just don't be mad at me if you get in trouble for missing curfew."

Said tag with action: "If you want to come," Kyle said, opening the car door, "get in, but don't be mad at me if you get in trouble for missing curfew."

Incorrect: "If you want to come," Kyle opened the car door, "get in, but don't be mad at me if you get in trouble for missing curfew."

That last example is incorrect because the inserted action is an independent clause stuck in the middle of another independent clause. Commas aren't strong enough to do the task without the help of a dialogue tag.

If you want to show action that is quickly interrupting dialogue, use em dashes. Since the break belongs to the sentence, however, rather than the dialogue inside, the em dashes must appear outside the quotation marks.

"If you want to come"—Kyle opened the car door—"get in, but don't be mad at me if you get in trouble for missing curfew."

Here are some more examples of using em dashes to interrupt dialogue with action.

"Before we start"—the knight plunged one of the blades into the grassy soil—"we need to go over the basics."

"With the casserole in to bake"—Rachel closed the oven door—"we will be ready to eat in twenty minutes."

You can also use em dashes to interrupt dialogue with a thought tag.

"I'm telling you"—and I can't believe I was going to admit this—"it was my fault."

Another way to write action interrupting that original sentence would be to divide it into two sentences.

Action tag: "If you want to come, get in." Kyle opened the car door. "But don't be mad at me if you get in trouble for missing curfew."

Whenever you divide a sentence of dialogue, make sure the division falls in a natural place for your character to pause. Read the dialogue out loud to see what sounds best.

15
Apostrophes

Apostrophes are used to mark the omission of letters or numbers. They also make a word possessive. Keep a close eye on your apostrophes. Word processing programs sometimes mistake them for single quotation marks and flip them the wrong way. Apostrophes should always curl this ' direction.

Use an apostrophe in contractions.

In a contraction, an apostrophe usually stands in the place of one or more letters that have been dropped. Words like *ain't* and *won't* are exceptions to that rule.

It's too early to go.
I can't believe you said that.
I don't want to go!
She's the best one for the job.
We should've bought the family-size bag.

Use an apostrophe to replace letters or numbers that have been omitted.

Authors use apostrophes to spell words or numbers in ways that show a character's accent.

The mistake I often see with this rule is backwards apostrophes. If your font uses straight quotes, this isn't an issue. But if your font uses curly quotes, make sure that the apostrophe curls in the right direction. The apostrophe is not a single quote. There is no reason for it to ever be backward. This can be tricky, as I mentioned before, because sometimes word processing programs flip that apostrophe around, which is frustrating. No matter if the apostrophe comes at the beginning of a word, in the middle, or at the end, it should always curl to the left: '

In the following example, the apostrophe takes the place of the *g* in "telling."

There be no tellin' what he'll do now.

In the next example, the letters *a* and *d* in the word "and" have been omitted. An apostrophe sits in the place of each missing letter.

All you kids do is sit around listening to that rock 'n' roll.

When more than one adjacent letter or number are omitted, use only one apostrophe to show what's missing. Below, the apostrophe takes the place of the *un* in the word "until." And in the second sentence, an apostrophe replaces the *th* in "them" and another apostrophe takes the place of the *h* in "here."

I won't come out 'til you promise not to laugh!
We got 'em right 'ere.

When you want to abbreviate a year or decade, use an apostrophe to replace the first two numbers. In the following examples, the apostrophe takes the place of the *19* in "1993" and 1990s.

I graduated high school in the class of '93.
Grunge music was popular in the '90s

Creating Possessive Nouns

To turn a singular noun into a possessive, add an apostrophe and an *s*, even if the noun ends in the letter *s*. A plural noun that ends in *s* requires an apostrophe only at the end to become plural. The same rules apply to creating possessives from numbers or abbreviations.

It's Billy's turn to ride the bike.
A Time to Kill was this reader's favorite book.
Oregon's beaches are breathtaking.
Chris's story is awesome!
"For Cetheira's hand, get in the tree!"[1]
Almost all of Jesus's disciples were loyal.
My mother-in-law's perfume is always toxic.
Massachusetts's population is growing.
"Gervais's homework is all turned in."
"I'll meet you in the girls' restroom after class."
The kittens' litterbox reeked.
The pirates' loot covered the deck of the ship.
All the production assistants' offices are down that hallway.
The children's playground was painted red and yellow.
"Are you going over to the Jensens' house?
"The Gowerses' fence is too tall for me to see the mountains.
The FBI's reputation is stellar.
DARE's website is down.
Apollo 13's mission was scary.

BOTH CORRECT?

Technically, words that end in *s* can be made possessive by adding an apostrophe and an s or by simply adding an apostrophe. Both are correct; however, since *The Chicago Manual of Style* recommends using an apostrophe and an s, and they are the reference for fiction in the publishing industry, I recommend the same. Each publisher will decide which style they prefer, but until you are told differently, you'd be wise to adhere to *The Chicago Manual of Style*.

Compound Possession with Linked Nouns

Two or more nouns are considered a single unit when they possess the same item. Only the final noun in the list requires the possessive form.

My grandma and grandpa's house sits on a lake.
The dog and cat's door is in the back of the house.
Mary-Kate and Ashley's movies make me laugh.
Portland and Vancouver's I5 bridge has terrible traffic.

When the items possessed are owned individually, both nouns require the possessive form.

My grandma's and grandpa's passports need to be renewed.
The dog's and cat's food dishes are in the entry way.
Mary-Kate's and Ashley's boyfriends are coming too.
Portland's and Vancouver's bridges have terrible traffic.

Do not use an apostrophe when pluralizing a decade, a century, or an abbreviation.

I often see apostrophes used when pluralizing decades or abbreviations. This is incorrect. Unless you are turning these into possessive forms, they should only have an *s* added without an apostrophe.

I grew up in the '80s and '90s.
The 1900s were filled with technological progress.
The university gave away twenty-seven PhDs this year.
I used to buy DVDs, but now I only watch movies online.
There are thousands of JPEGs on my computer.

Pluralizing a Singular Letter

When pluralizing a singular letter, use an apostrophe and an *s* to avoid the confusion of having misspelled a word.

"You'd better mind your p's and q's, young lady!"

Kim bolded all the letter a's in the paragraph.

WHEN TO PLURALIZE A SURNAME

When pluralizing a surname, never add an apostrophe. That would make the last name possessive, not plural.

It can be confusing to know whether to add an *s* or an *es* to the end of a last name to pluralize it. Here are the rules:

Add an *s* if the last name ends with *a, b, c, d, e, f, g, h* (except in the cases of last names ending in *ch* or *sh*), *i, j, k, l, m, n, o, p, q, r, t, u, v, w, y*.

Add an *es* if the last name ends with *s, x, z, ch, sh*.

16
Numbers

Numbers aren't used often in fiction, but when they are, they are often used incorrectly. The rules for numbers are fairly simple, however. Numbers can be written two ways: spelled out in letters (two) or written in numerals (2).

When to Spell Out Numbers

Spell out numbers one through one hundred, rounded numbers (hundreds, millions), and ordinal numbers (first, second, third). Spell out numbers in reference to age. Use numerals for all other numbers. Also, avoid starting sentences with numerals.

"She's ninety-six years old!"
"One, I can't understand why you hate me. And, two, I don't like you either."

"I need fifty copies of the flyer," Megan said.

There were 5,500 seats in the auditorium.

Michael crouched down. "There are millions of ants here!"

Thirteen days later, the letter came.

"I am seventeen years, eleven months, and twelve days old."[1]

Fractional Quantities of Large Numbers

When you have a fractional large number, numerals are used. Also, if there are two types of numbers in the same sentence, use numerals for consistency.

Approximately 7.4 billion people live on the earth.

Nonavian dinosaurs lived between 254 to 65.5 million years ago.

Numbers as Percentages

Use numerals for all numbers that are part of a percentage, except at the beginning of a sentence. Spell out the word percent unless stating a scientific or statistical fact. In that case, use the % symbol.

Most literary agents take a 15 percent commission.

I'd give them a 90 percent chance of success.

Twenty percent of my income goes to taxes.

My credit card has a 12.7 percent interest rate.

Only 20–35 percent of the attendees have been published.

The table shows that 18% of your students are planning to return to school next year.

When the experiment was repeated, 65% of the subjects were willing to obey instructions.

Ordinal Numbers

Ordinal numbers define a position in a series, such as *first*, *second*, *third*, etc. In most cases, you can spell out these numbers or use their abbreviated form (1st, 2nd, 3rd). Do not use superscript when using abbreviated forms.

"I'm first in line!"
Shelia lives on the twenty-second floor of the high rise.
Mark is ranked 114th overall.
My grandpa served in the 142nd Division.

Starting Sentences with Numbers

When a number or year begins a sentence, always spell it out rather than use numerals. If you prefer not to or the sentence sounds awkward, rewrite the sentence.

Twenty-four kids came to Johnny's birthday party.
Two thousand five hundred students attend Skyward High.
Skyward High has 2500 students.
Nineteen seventy-five was the year of my birth.
I was born in 1975.

Punctuating Time

Always spell out the time of day unless you're referring to the exact time, then use numerals. Use a.m. or p.m. with exact times.

Drew went to bed at five o'clock, exhausted from the tournament.
"Mom slept in, and I missed my nine-thirty appointment."
"I get to work early since the bus comes by at 7:10 a.m."
"Class starts at 8:35 tomorrow morning. Don't be late."

Punctuating Dates

Dates are written with numerals. Do not use ordinal numerals, though the dates may be pronounced as ordinals when reading aloud. Separate day and year numerals with a comma.

We moved on August 1.
"The photograph is copyright April 1942."
"On January 1, 2000, there were no major fallouts due to the new millennium."

When a day is mentioned without the month or year, spell out the number in ordinal form with letters, not numerals.

I was born on the sixth.
On the eighth of June, Mario and his family moved to America.
"By the fifteenth, finals will be over and we can focus on spring break."

Do not use an apostrophe when pluralizing a decade.

It is incorrect to use an apostrophe to pluralize decades or abbreviations.

Movies made in the 1980s are the best.
I grew up in the '80s and '90s.

Use numerals when referring to pages, chapters, or parts of a book.

See page 9 of this book to learn about appositives.
In Chapter 3, I discuss common mistakes in fiction.

17
Italics

Back in the days of the typewriter, there was no such thing as italics, so underlining was used to emphasize a word. Today, italics are used for emphasis. Do not use boldface, all caps, or underlining in your manuscript, unless you or your publisher have good reason.

Italics are also used for some interior dialogue, to specify foreign words, and to punctuate some titles.

Use italics to emphasize a word or phrase.

When you want the reader to give emphasis to a certain word or phrase, italicize the text. Some authors put the word or phrase in quotation marks, but that is incorrect.

I don't *think* so.
Mark didn't do it. *Shelia* did.

"Because I *said so*, Mark."
Mitty loved his family, but he didn't usually *notice*
  loving them.[1]
"She must be *made* to learn," her father said to Miss
  Minchin.[2]

The use of italics with interior dialogue.

While *The Chicago Manual of Style* does not recommend it, many publishers of fiction use italics without quotes to format direct thoughts or imagined dialogue, also called interior discourse. If you do this, do it rarely. Too much is a sign of amateur writing.

Some authors will put such thoughts in quotes without italics and use a dialogue tag such as "he thought" to mark how the words are to be read. Then there are the authors who use no special formatting at all.

Each publishing house has a style they prefer for showing inner discourse, and they will inform you of that during the editing phase. Depending on the publishing house, all of the following could be considered correct. Whichever style you choose, be consistent throughout your manuscript.

She skipped me, Jonas thought, stunned.[3]
Saints, she'd thought, *if he believes that, he really must
  be desperate*.[4]
"What is he doing?" Billy thought.
Where was he going? she wondered.

While the above examples are technically correct, you could also rewrite the sentence to avoid the need to mark interior discourse. This is my preferred method. Since we are in a point of view character's head, every word on the page is already his or her thoughts.

She skipped me. What the heck? Am I invisible?
Mike looked at his math test. He'd failed. He couldn't
believe it.
Where was he going?

Use italics to mark the use of a foreign word or phrase.

Foreign words or phrases should be italicized, unless they are found in Webster's dictionary or they are a proper noun. Also, if a foreign word is introduced and will be used repeatedly throughout the story, only italicize its first use; however, if the word will repeat only rarely, italicize it every time it is used.

"*Mais oui*, it is quite *différent*," the Hitler wannabe
said.[5]
"If *politsia* is stopping you, they are wanting to see
passport and visa."[6]
Isabel raised her eyebrows. "*Su familia?*"[7]
"*Yame!*" Kimura-san yelled.[8]
Can you say *abierto*?
"*Danke*," the woman said.
His name is Francois. (Not italicized, as Francois is a
proper noun.)
Have you been to Shanghai? (Not italicized, as
Shanghai is a proper noun.)

Use italics with titles of certain works.

Titles for books, newspapers, magazines, plays, movies, movie series, video games, and television, radio, or podcast programs are italicized. Only italicize the word *newspaper* or *magazine* if it is part of the title.

I wrote a book called *Captives*.
I still get the *Los Angeles Times* delivered to my door.
I cut up all my issues of *Vogue* magazine for class.
The play *Romeo and Juliet* doesn't have a happy
    ending.
Have you seen the movie *Christopher Robin*?
I love any *Star Trek* movie.
I used to love to play *Tetris* as a kid.
My son loves *Mario Bros.* video games.
The show *Chuck* cracks me up.
I've loved every season of *Blue Bloods*.
My kids never miss Focus on the Family's *Adventures
    in Odyssey* broadcast.
My husband has a podcast called *The Corner of
    Hollywood and Broadway*.

18
Capitalization

The Chicago Manual of Style has a huge section on the topic of capitalization. I'm going to try and keep things simple and only mention rules that apply to writing fiction or talking about fiction.

When to Capitalize

Capitalize names, nicknames, specific places, countries, planets, nationalities, religions, religious terms, months, days, holidays, organizations, departments, awards, and any other proper or specific noun.

My name is Jill.
His name is Badden, but we call him Buddy instead.
Because Mother said so.
I love Dad, don't you?
That car belongs to Grandpa Bill.
Greg, this is Aunt Shellie.
I love going to Jump Creek.

My parents went to Nicaragua.
Sometimes I can see Mars in the sky.
I've always wanted to see the Eiffel Tower.
Michelle is Canadian, and Josue is Guatemalan.
There are both Muslims and Christians in my school.
There is a new movie about the Norse god Thor.
Christians believe in God, Jesus, and the Holy Spirit.
David's family celebrates Passover.
I can't believe March is almost over.
This Friday is Thanksgiving day.
You could have a Christmas pageant without *any* baby
     angels, but you couldn't have one without a Mary.[1]
I am a member of Willamette Writers.
I applied for a business license from the Washington
     Department of Licensing.
I won a Christy Award.

Capitalize terms of respect.
Titles of honor are capitalized. All other general terms of respect are lowercase.

May I approach the bench, Your Honor?
Did you know His Highness likes beets?
Yes, Your Majesty.
We saw His Excellency, the Pope, outside the Vatican.
Yes, sir, I will.
No, ma'am. I didn't.
Will you come here, miss?
I serve my lord as best I can.
Did you know my lady Charlotte descends from Queen
     Victoria?

Words That Should Not Be Capitalized
Do not capitalize general, common nouns. Do not capitalize terms of endearment. Do not capitalize words like river, street, road, or

directions like south, northwest, or eastern unless they are part of a title or referring to a specific place.

Notice that some of the following examples are nearly the same sentences that I used on pages 102–103, but because in these examples the title (mom, dad, aunt, uncle, etc.) is preceded by a pronoun (my, our, his, her, their, etc.), they are lowercase.

"I love you, baby."
Because my mother said so.
I love our dad, don't you?
That car belongs to his grandpa Bill.
Greg, this is my aunt Shellie.
My parents went abroad.
Sometimes I can see the moon in the sky.
We like to throw stones in the river.
I live right behind the Little Susitna River.
Did you know that Bliss and Martinson roads run parallel to one another?
Drive northwest out of town and you'll find the barn.
Michael moved here from eastern Idaho.
It's so hot in the South.

Capitalize the words *a*, *an*, or *the* when they begin a book title.

The Chicago Manual of Style recommends you capitalize the words *a*, *an*, or *the* when such words begin a title. It is acceptable to drop these words, however, when it better fits the surrounding syntax.

I love the book *A Walk to Remember*.
I wrote *The New Recruit*.
Williamson's *New Recruit* follows Spencer Garmond
    on a training mission to Moscow.

What to Capitalize in a Work's Title

For titles of books, chapters, songs, and poems, the rules are as follows.

The following are always capitalized:
1. The first and the last word in a title.
2. All nouns, pronouns, verbs, adjectives, and adverbs.
3. Subordinating conjunctions *as, if, when, so, because, that, than*. (*She's So Unusual*). For a list of subordinating conjunctions, see page 8.
4. The first world following a colon or dash (*Replication: The Jason Experiment*).

The following are always lowercased:
1. Articles *a, an*, and *the*, except when it's the first or last word of the title (*An Officer and a Gentleman*).
2. Coordinating conjunctions *and, but, for, or, nor* (*Eleanor and Park*).
3. Prepositions *through, up, down, on, by, in, of, with, to* (*Anne of Avonlea*), except when they are used as an adverb or adjective (*White House Down*).
4. The words *to* and *as* (*Bridge to Terabithia*), unless they are the first or last word in the title (*As the World Turns*), unless

to is used in a verb phrase (*To Be or Not To Be*), or unless *as* is a subordinating conjunction (*For As Long As We Both Shall Live*).

5. The part of a proper name that is normally lowercase (*van* or *de la*).

19
Scene Breaks and Section Breaks

Have you ever been reading a book and noticed that sometimes a break in a scene is depicted by asterisks or some other fancy symbol(s), and sometimes there is only a large empty space before a new scene begins? The former is marking a section break and the latter is marking a scene break.

Use asterisks, bullets, or a number sign to mark a section break.
A section break is used to indicate the end of a scene or a change in point of view character.

A section break is made by hitting enter to leave one blank line, centering on the next line the same amount of asterisks or bullets (either with no spaces between them or with the same number of spaces between them) or a single number sign, then hitting enter to leave another blank line, then hitting enter again to start typing a new paragraph.

In the following example from an early draft of my novel *The New Recruit*, you can see how the section break separated two different scenes.

"... Try to hold tightly to your temper when you are playing the sport of basketball *à la gym*. This I know is strange to hear, but sometimes these things come to me. In my dreams." Prière tapped his temple. "Think about my warning, *oui*?"

The dude was dreaming about me? Creepy.

* * *

At lunch the next day, everyone had already heard what had happened with Nick. The Mission League kids had infiltrated the basketball table ... again. I really wasn't in the mood to deal with them, Isabel excepted.

Before the section break, Prière, a prophet, is trying to give Spencer a warning. The blank lines and asterisks show the reader that the scene ended. What comes after is the start of the next scene.

Be consistent in the way you indicate a section break.

Whether you choose to use asterisks, bullets (with spaces, tabs, or no spaces), or a single number sign doesn't matter, as long as you consistently do the same thing for every section break in your manuscript. Consistency is the mark of a professional. Here are some variations of acceptable ways to indicate a section break.

```
****
*          *          *
•      •   •
•••
• • •
#
```

THE NUMBER SIGN

A single number sign, also called the pound sign or hashtag, can be used to indicate a section break.

If you choose to use the number sign, I recommend using only one per section break since three centered number signs are often used to indicate the end of a novel.

It might confuse editors or make you look like an amateur if you use three number signs at every section break.

Don't use fancy graphics, clip art, or decorative symbols to mark section breaks.

I know it's tempting to want to make your manuscript look like a typeset novel, but if you're formatting a manuscript to submit to a literary agent or an editor at a publishing house, getting creative in this area will mark you an amateur. Stick with asterisks or bullets and you will be safe. It's the publisher's job to typeset the novels they produce.

If you're self-publishing, however, that's another story. Since you will be the publisher, you can choose whatever kind of decorative symbol you want. You will be in complete control of your finished product.

Use two blank lines to mark a scene break.

A scene break is a separation between the same scene. It's used to indicate time passing or a change of location that continues within the same scene.

A scene break is created when you hit enter (or return) three times in a double-spaced document, leaving two blank lines between one section of text and the next section of text.

In the following example, also from my novel *The New Recruit*, you can see how the scene break shows that time has passed.

"You believe in angels and demons?" [Isabel asked.]

"I guess."

"Ees real, Es-pensor." She turned back and opened her book again.

I wanted to say, "Don't go!" but all I could do was settle back in my seat and try to think of another question to ask.

Claustrophobia. I'd never understood the full meaning of that word until now. Coach seats were not meant for guys over six feet tall. At least I had the aisle to stretch my right leg, and I'd gotten up and walked to the restroom so many times I'd likely paved a groove into the floor.[1]

In the scene above, Spencer is on an airplane, talking to a pretty girl. The conversation ended, some time passed—indicated by the scene break—and when we return, Spencer is still on the airplane.

Starting a new chapter can indicate a section break *or* a scene break.

Starting a new chapter by inserting a page break can be another way to show the passing of time within the same scene or to begin a completely new scene—though many authors use chapter endings as cliffhangers, to keep readers turning the pages.

WHEN I BROKE THE RULES

I have always used three or four asterisks or bullets to mark both scene breaks and section breaks in my manuscripts. Some of my editors have changed out my scene breaks during the editing process. Some haven't.

As long as you are consistent in what you do in this area, editors and agents won't be bothered.

PART 2

Everything Else

20
Asterisks

Asterisks can be used in fiction as a footnote* to indicate a comment in the footer of the page. Two great examples of fiction that uses footnotes are Jonathan Stroud's *Bartimaeus Trilogy* and Susanna Clarke's *Jonathan Strange and Mr. Norrell*. Grab one of them and see what you think.

Asterisks also can be used to mark a section break in a novel, which I talked about in-depth in Chapter 19.

Some authors use asterisks to mark omitted letters of an expletive, i.e., d***, but *The Chicago Manual of Style*[1] recommends the 2-em dash for that purpose (see page 60). This is one rule you can get away with breaking, however. If a publishing house wants you to format it differently, they will tell you, but they would never reject you for using asterisks to sanitize swear words, as long as you do so sparingly.

---

*When using an asterisk to indicate a footnote, do not leave a space between the asterisk and the word it follows. Also, be sure to format the asterisk in superscript, which is usually a box you can select from the font menu.

If you are sanitizing swear words every-other page, don't. Choose what type of story you're telling and for what type of audience, then spell out those swear words or rewrite your material to avoid using them at all.

21
Parentheses

Using parentheses ( ) to set off information by way of explanation is rare in novels because it is "telling" rather than "showing." Parentheses can also be obtrusive and have the tendency to pull the reader out of the story.

Most editors frown on the use of parentheses in fiction manuscripts, unless using them fits the genre of the story, the style of the writing, and/or the voice of the narrator. Using parentheses can work well in some first-person stories, especially those written in a journal or letter format.

Use parentheses to set off parenthetical information.

Parentheses can be used to make explanations, translations, comments, or asides to the reader. Such information can often be set apart with commas or em dashes as well, but parentheses tend to be used when the enclosed information is not grammatically necessary to the surrounding sentence but you want to include it anyway.

If a sentence or fragment inside parentheses falls inside another complete sentence, don't capitalize the first letter of the parenthetical statement or add punctuation to the end, unless it is a question mark or exclamation point.

Now, if I manage to pass this test (yeah, right), I'll be able to apply for the scholarship.

Everyone was staring at Josh's new car (Porsche).

Michelle has three children (two girls and a boy), but on Wednesdays she also watches her sister's son.

She told him over dinner all about Mrs. Next Door's problems with her daughter and how Dudley had learned a new word ("Won't!").[1]

They went to dinner at Monte's (not too shabby, Mr. G!) and then walked around the West Village and went to some bar and sat outside in the back garden until nearly two in the morning, just talking.[2]

With a bored (yet artfully haughty) glance at the house I mutter, "It's okay."[3]

Did she buy that dress (the red one with the pleats)?

Taking a deep breath (because you never know what the air quality will be like), I opened the door and claimed my stall.[4]

A page break (code in an electronic document that sends succeeding information to a new page) is inserted into a manuscript before starting a new chapter.

The author used the Hebrew word for land (*er'rets*) to name her fantasy storyworld.

He introduced them as his *otosan* (father) and *okasan* (mother). They were both short and brown and full of smiles.[5]

Use parentheses to enclose a letter, a number, or a symbol when used as an appositive.

There were five (5) people initiated into the sorority last week.
Remember to use a percent (%) sign with any answers that require it.

Use parentheses to enclose letters or numbers that mark divisions in a run-in list.

As opposed to a horizontal list, a run-in list is part of a sentence. When you use letters or numbers in such lists, set them apart in parentheses. Precede run-in lists with a colon only if the introductory material forms a complete sentence.

While you are in the woods, you must (a) find a fresh water source, (b) find a food source, and (c) create a shelter.
Please bring the following items: (1) a laptop, (2) a notebook, (3) a writing utensil, and (4) a cell phone.

Parentheses with Other Punctuation

If the parenthetical information comes within a sentence, the punctuation to end the sentence goes outside the closing parenthesis.

I told him (whispering), just like you said.

Michael is a senior (just like Josh Richter). Michael has gotten all straight A's his entire life (just like Josh Richter). Michael will probably go to Yale or Harvard next year (just like Josh Richter).[6]

He asked me (can you believe it?) if I wanted to dance.

I have completed my epic saga (hooray!), and *Onyx Eyes* is still calling to me.

I went to the grocery store for taco ingredients (ground beef, refried beans, taco seasoning, tortilla shells, cheese, etc.).

If the parenthetical information stands on its own, the punctuation to end the sentence goes within the closing parenthesis.

All eyes were on me. (Okay, maybe five or six people stopped eating their burritos long enough to look my way, but it felt like two hundred.)[7]

My daughter was still watching YouTube. (The new laptop she got for Christmas was causing more problems than it was worth.)

And I also love this longer example from Meg Cabot's *The Princess Diaries*.[8]

Lilly intends to take a handheld camera down to Washington Square Park and film the tourists who come up to us and ask if we know how to get to Green Witch Village. (It's actually Greenwich Village—you're not supposed to pronounce the *w* in Greenwich. But people from out of town always say it wrong.)

22
Brackets

Square brackets [ ] (as opposed to angled brackets < >) are used for two common reasons. First, brackets are necessary when you need to use parentheses inside something that is already in parentheses. Second, brackets are used when someone besides the original author adds content to quoted material.

Use brackets to mark parentheses within parentheses.

I was running late (I couldn't find my keys [or my shoes!]), and my son would be standing outside his school in the rain, waiting.

Use brackets for missing, illegible, or guessed words when reproducing a quotation or to clarify content in a quotation that is ambiguous or unclear.

When you don't know part of a quotation or need to add or insert a word for clarity, you must indicate your changes with brackets. If you take out part of a quotation, use ellipses to show missing words. (See pages 63-65.)

The girl wiggled, then ran out of the door, headed for the [bathroom?].
On the third of June, I met with Suzanne who told me the secret of the treasure map would be found in the . . . [illegible] of Houston, Texas.
Today I went to sch[ool] with my [neigh]bor Marcus VanBu[ren].
The Houston Hawks defeated the Palmer Moose by only 2 [points].

In the publishing industry, brackets are often used to shorten endorsements. Below is an endorsement I received from *Library Journal* for my book *By Darkness Hid*.

In this medieval fantasy debut, idealistic servant Achan Cham dreams of becoming a Kingsguard Knight, while Vrell Sparrow disguises herself as a boy to escape an arranged marriage. She has a supernatural gift of being able to communicate to Achan without words. This thoroughly entertaining and smart tale will appeal to fans of Donita K. Paul and J.R.R. Tolkien. Highly recommended for CF and fantasy collections.

That's long to put on a book cover, so it was shortened to this.

"[T]horoughly entertaining and smart . . . [W]ill appeal to fans of Donita K. Paul and J.R.R. Tolkien. Highly recommended . . ."!

23
Slashes

There are two kinds of slashes, the forward slash / and the backslash \. Backslashes are mainly used in coding. It's the forward slash that we are going to discuss in regards to fiction. It shares the same key on a keyboard with the question mark.

Use a slash to show an alternative.
A slash can be a shorthand symbol for *and/or* and sometimes the word *or* alone. The pairings should be connected or conflicting.

Every student must bring a notebook/laptop.
If/when I graduate, I plan to backpack in Europe.
I work out of my den/home office.
The Seattle/Tacoma train leaves in an hour.
This is a pass/fail test.
I can't make sense of his rabbit/hare demeanor.

To be honest, I would never use a slash in fiction unless it fit my character's voice. In that case, I'd rather write something like "It was a kitchen-slash-dining area" than writing "It was a kitchen/dining area" because there's no guarantee a reader will pronounce the word *slash* in their heads just from seeing the punctuation mark.

If you want to show an alternative, that's fine, but if you can't decide which word is better or you want to use two words, remember that $1 + 1 = 1/2$. Being an author is all about choosing the best word for every circumstance. So, I recommend that you make a choice and pick the word that best fits the situation.

However, here is an example of using the slash for this very reason from Suzanne Collins's *The Hunger Games*.[1] As I mentioned at the start of this book, even bestselling novelists break rules, sometimes on purpose, sometimes not. While I think Ms. Collins likely wrote this as a form of irony, in my opinion, the word *prison* alone would have done the same task and packed a more ironic punch.

> The ride lasts about twenty minutes and ends up at the City Circle, where they will welcome us, play the anthem, and escort us into the Training Center, which will be our home/prison until the Games begin.

PART 3
The Art of Punctuating

24
Proofreading Marks

Authors don't receive many hand-written edits these days. Edits are usually done with Microsoft Word's Track Changes, but in the event you receive any physical pages with copyediting, here is a list of what some of the most common proofreading marks mean.

Delete	Mark is an excellent excellent basketball player.
Spelling error	Mark is an excellent basketball playar.
Capitalize	mark is an excellent basketball player.
Lowercase	Mark is an excellent Basketball player.
Add	Mark is a excellent basketball player.
Add a space	Mark isan excellent basketball player.
Add a period	Mark is an excellent basketball player
Change order	Mark an is excellent basketball player.
Close gap	Mark is an excellent basket ball player.
Delete and close gap	Mark Wilson is an excellent basketball player.
Meaning unclear	Mark is an excellent basketball.
Start a new paragraph	Mark is an excellent basketball player.

25
Going Deeper

You can be totally black and white about following every punctuation and grammar rule and write an entertaining book. You can also break lots of rules and still write an entertaining book. You, the author—the artist—get to decide what kind of author you are going to be.

And that's pretty exciting.

If writing is an art form, punctuation is a medium on your artist's palette. You could try and tell stories without any punctuation, but that would be like trying to paint without a canvas. Punctuation holds all your words together on the page. What's cool, though, is that no other author will use punctuation exactly like you.

Examine Your Methods

Have you ever seen the posters that strip classic novels down to their punctuation? I find it fascinating. For fun, I went ahead and did just that for my first published novel *By*

Darkness Hid and for Jane Austen's *Sense and Sensibility*. I first deleted out all the letters, formatting, and spaces until only the punctuation remained, then I pulled a random selection from each book and made an image to share. Here are my results.

By *Darkness Hid* by Jill Williamson

Sense and Sensibility by Jane Austen

Jane used many more commas than I did, a sign that she wrote more complex sentence structures. She also liked the occasional semicolon, em dash, and parentheses. And look at all those exclamation points!

I used shorter, simpler sentences. I also used lots of question marks and dialogue. Some of my question marks and quotation marks were italicized, which was how I formatted telepathic dialogue. (I'm a fantasy novelist.) I also had four section breaks in this image, each depicted by sets of three asterisks.

Isn't that fun?

Here is how I did this. Using the Find and Replace function in Microsoft Word, I replaced one letter and numeral at a time with nothing in the replace box. This is basically going through and deleting the letter As, then the letter Bs, etc., all the way through the alphabet. I did the same for each numeral (0–9). Then I deleted all the spaces. And finally I had to delete all the formatting by looking up the following symbols and replacing them with nothing:

^p for paragraphs, ^t for tabs, ^l for line breaks, and ^k for page breaks.

It was tedious, let me tell you. Once I was done, I copied-and-pasted a section of the punctuation into Photoshop, but you could paste it into Paint or any other graphics art program. Then I had to manually hit "enter" at the end of every line to make the punctuation fill the page.

You don't have to go this far to examine your punctuation methods, but do study them. Why do you do what you do? Do you have a reason? Or do you choose your punctuation without really thinking about it? Is there a particular punctuation mark that you overuse? Is there one you rarely or never use?

Experiment

How might changing some of the punctuation marks, varying the sentence structure, or using more or less dialogue or paragraphs in your writing impact the stories you tell?

Record yourself reading some of your writing out loud, then play it back. Do you hear a rhythm to your words? Is your prose short and choppy or does it ebb and flow? Does your pacing barrel forward like a freight train or does it meander along like a man on a leisurely stroll? Do you have a good contrast of both? How are your transitions? Do you switch starkly from one to another, do you prolong action to create tension, or do you gradually build up to a magnificent crescendo?

How do your sentence structures work together? Would you read a sentence differently if you rewrote it? Broke it down into shorter sentences? Combined it with some other sentences? Added more commas? Turned some of your dialogue into narrative or your narrative into dialogue? What if you replaced some of your commas with em dashes?

Play around with this and see what you discover. The slightest changes here and there could affect the way your story looks, sounds, and feels to a reader.

Find Your Unique Style

It will take time and practice to find your unique writing style. This is one reason I encourage new writers to set aside that first manuscript that has so dazzled them and write a second book. Then a third, fourth, and fifth book. With each new book, you improve in craft, style, and voice. You hone your skills.

While you're writing, it might be fun to study the punctuation practices of other writers. Don't read only in your genre, though. Read widely, in many genres, including poetry, which is a genre that uses punctuation in many creative ways.

Practice, learn, and grow. Once the rules become second nature, you'll no longer worry if you can get away with breaking them. Your respect for the rules, your instincts, and your experience will make all this second nature. You'll know, deep down, that no one else in the world can tell a story like you can.

Selected Bibliography

Listed below are books that I consulted during the writing of this project and some I simply enjoy.

For those looking to learn more or increase their reference collection, I highly recommend all these resources and anything else these authors might have penned on the subject of grammar and punctuation.

What I could not list are textbooks, courses, workshops, and writer's conferences I have learned from over the course of my life and career. Nor am I able to credit every editor, agent, and author who mentored me along the way. I have learned much from so many and am grateful.

Browne, R., and Dave King. *Self-Editing for Fiction Writers*. 2nd ed. New York: HarperCollins, 2004.

Cochrane, J. *Between You and I: A Little Book of Bad English*. Naperville: Sourcebooks, 2004

Dictionary.com. https://dictionary.com

The Editor's Blog. http://theeditorsblog.net

Grammar Girl. https://www.quickanddirtytips.com/grammar-girl

Grammarly. https://www.grammarly.com

Merriam-Webster, Incorporated. *Merriam-Webster's Collegiate Dictionary*. 11th ed. Springfield: Merriam-Webster, 2003.

O'Conner, P. *Woe Is I: A Grammaphobe's Guide to Better English in Plain English*. New York: Riverhead Books, 1996.

Shaw, H. *Punctuate It Right!* New York: Harper Paperbacks, 1993.

Strunk, W., and E. B. White. *The Elements of Style: 50th Anniversary Edition*. New York: Pearson Longman, 2009.

Walsh, B. *The Elephants of Style: A Trunkload of Tips on the Big Issues and Gray Areas of Contemporary American English*. New York: McGraw-Hill, 2004.

Walsh, B. *Lapsing Into a Comma: A Curmudgeon's Guide to the Many Things That Can Go Wrong in Print—and How to Avoid Them*. New York: McGraw-Hill, 2000.

University of Chicago Press. *The Chicago Manual of Style*. 17th ed. Chicago: University of Chicago Press, 2017.

Notes

Chapter 2: Some Basics

1. George MacDonald, *The Princess and the Goblin* (London: Puffin Books, a division of Penguin Random House, 2010), 116.

2. Robert Cormier, *The Chocolate War* (New York: Laurel Leaf Books, a division of Dell Publishing, Co., Inc., 1986), 8.

3. Kate DiCamillo, *Because of Winn Dixie* (Cambridge: Candlewick Press, 2001), 57.

Chapter 3: Common Mistakes in Fiction

1. Charles Dickens, *A Tale of Two Cities* (New York: Bantam Books, 1981), 1.

Chapter 4: Periods

1. Douglas Adams, *The Hitchhiker's Guide to the Galaxy* (New York: Pocket Books, a Simon & Schuster division of Gulf & Western Corporation, 1979), 3.

2. Beverly Cleary, *Beezus and Ramona* (New York: Avon Camelot, a division of The Hearst Corporation, 1990), 1.

3. L. M. Montgomery, *Anne of Green Gables* (Toronto: Seal Books, division of McClelland-Bantam, Inc., 1981), 26.

4. Meg Cabot, *The Princess Diaries* (New York: HarperTrophy, an imprint of HarperCollins Publishers, 2000), 10.

Chapter 5: Question Marks

1. DiCamillo, *Because of Winn Dixie*, 7.
2. Janet Evanovich, *One for the Money* (New York: St. Martin's Paperbacks Edition, 2003), 18.
3. Montgomery, *Anne of Green Gables*, 24.

Chapter 6: Exclamation Points

1. Montgomery, *Anne of Green Gables*, 23.
2. Cabot, *The Princess Diaries*, 89.

Chapter 7: Commas

1. MacDonald, *The Princess and the Goblin*, 40.
2. MacDonald, *The Princess and the Goblin*, 113.
3. Suzanne Collins, *The Hunger Games* (New York: Scholastic Press, 2008), 101.
4. Caroline B. Cooney, *Code Orange* (New York: Laurel Leaf Books, a division of Random House, Inc., 2005), 42.
5. Lois Lowry, *The Giver* (New York: Laurel Leaf Books, a division of Random House, Inc., 2002), 22.
6. Jerry Spinelli, *Stargirl*, (Scholastic, 2002), 30.
7. Lowry, *The Giver*, 1.
8. Anne Frank, *The Diary of a Young Girl* (New York: Bantam Books, 1993), 59.
9. Collins, *The Hunger Games*, 134.
10. Evanovich, *One for the Money*, 175.
11. Lowry, *The Giver*, 7.
12. Cormier, *The Chocolate War*, 61.

Chapter 8: Colons

1. J. K. Rowling, *Harry Potter and the Sorcerer's Stone* (New York: Scholastic Press, 1998), 37.
2. Mark Twain, *The Adventures of Tom Sawyer* (New York: Bantam Dell, a division of Random House Inc., 2004), 45.

Chapter 9: Semicolons

1. Jill Williamson, *Replication: The Jason Experiment* (Grand Rapids: Zondervan, 2011) 22.

Chapter 10: Dashes

1. Rowling, *Harry Potter and the Sorcerer's Stone*, 171.

2. Frank Capra and James Stewart, *It's a Wonderful Life* (Los Angeles, CA: Liberty Films, 1946).

3. Sir Arthur Conan Doyle, *The Hound of the Baskervilles* (New York, Berkley Medallion Books, 1971), 84.

Chapter 11:Ellipses

1. Rowling, *Harry Potter and the Sorcerer's Stone*, 290.

2. John Grisham, *The Firm* (New York: Doubleday, a division of Bantam Doubleday Dell Publishing Group, Inc., 1991), 327.

Chapter 12: Hyphens

1. J. R. R. Tolkien, *The Hobbit* (New York: a Del Ray Book, published by the Ballentine Publishing Group, a division of Random House, Inc., 1982), 17.

2. Rowling, *Harry Potter and the Sorcerer's Stone*, 68.

3. Evanovich, *One for the Money*, 33.

4. MacDonald, *The Princess and the Goblin*, 149.

Chapter 13: Quotation Marks

1. Jill Williamson, *The New Recruit* (Colorado Springs: Marcher Lord Press, 2012), 73.

2. Cormier, *The Chocolate War*, 80.

3. Spinelli, *Stargirl*, 78.

4. Jill Williamson, *Chokepoint* (Vancouver: Novel Teen Press, 2012), 30.

Chapter 14: Dialogue Tags

1. Jill Williamson, *THIRST*, (Vancouver: Novel Teen Press, 2016), http://jillwilliamson.com/2016/02/thirst-chapter-one/.

2. Collins, *The Hunger Games*, 134.

3. Lowry, *The Giver*, 18.

4. Cooney, *Code Orange*, 127.

5. Cabot, *The Princess Diaries*, 225.

Chapter 15: Apostrophes

1. Jill Williamson, *By Darkness Hid* (Colorado Springs: Marcher Lord Press, 2009), 338.

Chapter 16: Numbers

1. Williamson, *Replication: The Jason Experiment*, 97.

Chapter 17: Italics

1. Cooney, *Code Orange*, 86.

2. Frances Hodges Burnett, *The Little Princess* (New York: HarperCollins Publishers, 1999), 31.

3. Lowry, *The Giver*, 57.

4. Leigh Bardugo, *Six of Crows* (New York: Henry Holt and Company, 2015) 62.

5. Williamson, *The New Recruit*, 13.

6. Williamson, *The New Recruit*, 141.

7. Williamson, *The New Recruit*, 181.

8. Jill Williamson, *Project Gemini* (Colorado Springs: Marcher Lord Press, 2013), 127.

Chapter 18: Capitalization

1. Barbara Robinson, *The Best Christmas Pageant Ever* (New York: Scholastic, 2009), 36.

Chapter 19: Scene Breaks Vs. Section Breaks

1. Jill Williamson, *The New Recruit* (Colorado Springs: Marcher Lord Press, 2012), 122.

Chapter 20: Asterisks

1. University of Chicago Press, *The Chicago Manual of Style* (Chicago: University of Chicago Press, 2017), 401.

Chapter 21: Parentheses

1. Rowling, *Harry Potter and the Sorcerer's Stone*, 6.
2. Cabot, *The Princess Diaries*, 17.
3. Jenny B. Jones, *In* Between (Colorado Springs, NavPress, 2007), 22.
4. Jones, *In Between*, 182.
5. Jill Williamson, *Project Gemini* (Colorado Springs, Marcher Lord Press, 2013), 88.
6. Cabot, *The Princess Diaries*, 10.
7. Jones, *In Between*, 183.
8. Cabot, *The Princess Diaries*, 18.

Chapter 23: The Slash

1. Collins, *The Hunger Games*, 69.

Index

To learn more, visit www.JillWilliamson.com/books

About The Author

Jill Williamson has written over twenty books for teens and adults, including her debut novel, *By Darkness Hid*, which won several awards and was named a Best Science Fiction, Fantasy, and Horror novel of 2009 by *VOYA* magazine. She has written several books on the craft of writing fiction and teaches writing in person and online at storyworldfirst.com and at goteenwriters.com, the latter of which has been named one of Writer's Digest's "101 Best Websites for Writers." To learn more, visit her online at jillwilliamson.com.

AWARD-WINNING FANTASY
FROM JILL WILLIAMSON

"Wonderfully written with a superb plot, this book is a sure-fire hit with almost any reader. An adventure tale with a touch of romance and enough intrigue to keep the pages turning practically by themselves."
—*VOYA* magazine

"This thoroughly entertaining and smart tale will appeal to fans of Donita K. Paul and J.R.R. Tolkien. Highly recommended for . . . fantasy collections."
—*Library Journal*

"Williamson crafts a complex and vividly portrayed epic fantasy reminiscent of George R.R. Martin's *A Song of Ice and Fire* series but less edgy."
—*Library Journal*

"[*King's Folly*] is an intense drama of biblical proportions... Wilek, Mielle, and Trevn in particular are intriguing, and the ending leaves readers wondering what adventures await this group of young people searching for truth."
—*RT Book Reviews*

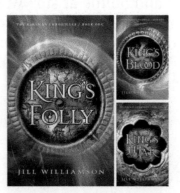

TO LEARN MORE VISIT
WWW.JILLWILLIAMSON.COM

MORE WRITING RESCOURCES FROM JILL WILLIAMSON

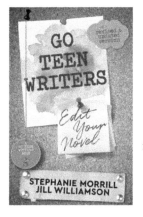

REVISED & UPDATED EDITION!

You know your first draft has problems, but what's the best way to fix them? How do you know where to start editing? Or for many writers the bigger question becomes, "How do I know when I'm done?"

Teaching yourself how to edit a first draft can feel overwhelming, but using this guide, you'll feel as encouraged, empowered, and capable as if you had a writing coach sitting alongside you.

BUILDING A STORYWORLD? WONDERING WHERE TO START? THIS BOOK CAN HELP YOU.

Whether you're starting from scratch or looking to add depth to a world you've already created, *Storyworld First* will get you thinking.

Includes tips on the following worldbuilding subjects: astronomy, magic, government, map-making, history, religion, technology, languages, culture, and how it all works together.

TO LEARN MORE VISIT
WWW.JILLWILLIAMSON.COM

Lightning Source UK Ltd.
Milton Keynes UK
UKHW020723150819
347977UK00008B/1346/P